Solomon Schindler

Messianic Expectations and Modern Judaism

Solomon Schindler

Messianic Expectations and Modern Judaism

ISBN/EAN: 9783337338107

Printed in Europe, USA, Canada, Australia, Japan

Cover: Foto ©Lupo / pixelio.de

More available books at **www.hansebooks.com**

Messianic Expectations

AND

Modern Judaism.

LECTURES DELIVERED BY

Solomon Schindler,

OF THE TEMPLE ADATH ISRAEL, IN BOSTON.

With an Introduction by

Minot J. Savage.

Boston:
S. E. CASSINO AND COMPANY.
1886.

COPYRIGHT, 1886,
BY S. E. CASSINO AND COMPANY.

ELECTROTYPED BY
C. J. PETERS & SON, BOSTON.

TO

𝔐𝔶 𝔅𝔢𝔩𝔬𝔳𝔢𝔡 𝔚𝔦𝔣𝔢,

HENRIETTE SCHINDLER,

THIS BOOK IS DEDICATED IN
THANKFULNESS,

BY THE AUTHOR.

PREFACE.

"WHAT epoch would you choose to have lived in?" a lady once asked the late Chauncey Wright. "The most modern," was his reply. Amen, say I, unless I could come to life again in a hundred or a thousand years. For the present most certainly is the most cheering and inspiring age of the world's history so far. The world is not old, worn out, and hastening to decay. Politically, industrially, and religiously, we are seeing the first rays of the dawn of humanity's long day. The real "Golden Age" is ahead of us, not in the past. The twilight has been very long; and, while the mists and shadows have hung over the earth, people have easily imagined faces of hate and terror looking down on them out of the sky, and have found it hard to recognize friends in the uncertain movements of those about them. But now that the sun is up, the sky is seen to smile, and the supposed enemies of the darkness are found to be friends.

One of the most striking indications of this religious advance is the coming together at last of the Christian and the Jew. According to the narrow "orthodox" interpretation of these words this coming together may seem to be brought about by the Christian's ceasing to be a Christian, and the Jew's ceasing to be a Jew. But if so, it is only because those terms have been so interpreted as to be too small for the growing religious life of man. If either "Christian" or "Jew" is so defined as to make it less than "man," then it is time for both of them to be outgrown.

And it is curious and instructive to note the genesis of the old hate as well as the genesis of the new friendship. The Jews, at the time of their captivity in Babylon, borrowed the story of Eden and the Fall of Man from an old Turanian epic. And this, together with their own traditions, which they came to regard as the infallible Word of God, became the instrument of their bondage, and the means of their isolation from the common life of humanity. This same book also, supplemented by another Scripture, and interpreted in the light of that other, became also the mental prison-house of Christendom. And this isolation in both cases bred spiritual pride and hate.

But now, after long centuries of enmity, at least some Christians and some Jews have grown brave enough to question their traditions. They dare to be hospitable to new ideas, to think that even the religious world may become wiser, and that maturity may know more than childhood. So, as they look into each other's faces, they are becoming conscious that religious hate was born of religious ignorance and conceit, and that a truer knowledge of God means a broader love for man.

Thus when Jew and Christian cease fighting over what neither of them knows, they find themselves on the common ground of human need, human labor, and human hope. And here God meets them as the common Father and Helper.

This volume of lectures by a Jew, delivered to an audience more than half of which was Christian, and treating frankly and freshly a theme of equal interest to both, is both prophecy and fulfilment of the broader religious life of the time. As such I hail it. My standing here to introduce my friend to a larger audience than that which first greeted him does not mean that I am ready to agree with everything he says. It means a much better thing than that—the grand and hopeful fact that the world at last is willing to hear an earnest man without waiting to find out whether it agrees with him or not. We are coming to have faith in truth at last; and this is much better than believing that our faith is true. Having got rid of the conceit that we already have all the truth that God intended for the world, there is some hope now of our really finding all the truth we need. I welcome this book because I believe that it is at least honest in its search. And since the truth-seeker is the only God-seeker, I feel sure that they who seek shall find the Father.

But now my simple task is done. An architect once said to me, many years ago, "Columns that support nothing, but are set up only to look at, are bad taste in architecture. Have only what is of use; then ornament that as much as you please." I have often thought of this as applying in general to all literary style. And particularly have I thought of it when called on to write a preface to a book. This book needs no columns of mine to support it. It will be able to stand on its own foundations. And I should regard it as specially bad taste in me to set up too long a row of pillars in front of it. My only ambition has been to set up a few very modest posts to mark the path that leads to the doorway, and thus to indicate my belief that it will be worth the reader's while to enter in.

M. J. SAVAGE.

FEB. 18, 1886.

CONTENTS.

	PAGE
Introductory	1
"Two Thousand Years Ago"	15
"The Carpenter's Son"	32
Judaism the Mother, Christianity the Daughter	50
A Genuine Messiah	66
The Spanish Inquisition	83
David Rubeni and Solomon Molcho	101
The Kabbalah	118
Sabbatai Zwi	134
Conclusion	152

The Pittsburg Conference: Its Causes	170
The Pittsburg Conference: Its Work	186
Modern Judaism	206
The Sinaitic Revelation	224
Moses	239
Propagation of Religion	256
Churches and their Relation to Morals	276

MESSIANIC EXPECTATIONS.

I.

INTRODUCTORY.

IDEAS are as mortal as men, who are their exponents: their origin and life are similar to that of any human being: they are limited, as is mankind, by time and space. Ideas are first conceived by the human mind, and pass a period of embryonic existence before they become strong enough to bear the light and the changing temperature of the world. Then they pass a term of childhood, during which they are subject to all kinds of diseases, and the weak among them die fast, like infants in a crowded city. Those only which are endowed with sufficient vitality survive; they grow up to manhood, fight their battles, and not seldom conquer the world. After their mission is fulfilled and their vitality exhausted, they enter into a period of decrepit old age. Though they are now of little, if any, usefulness, they still command the respect and the reverence of the world on account of their age and their former renown. But every day brings them nearer to the grave, until their last hour strikes; and after a few last convulsions they pass away, sometimes as unnoticed as they appeared upon the stage of life.

Before, however, their contemporaries are ready to bury them, a dispute frequently arises as to the reality of their death. Some can hardly believe that an idea which has lived and worked among them for such a length of time, which has performed such great and marvellous deeds, and which has commanded their reverence during all their lifetime, has indeed passed away. They cling to it with filial love and devotion, and deceive themselves with the hope that the departed idea is only asleep for a while, or in a trance from which it will surely awaken after a few hours. Others, who have always been depending on the departed idea for their sustenance, are fearing the loss of their support, and are unwilling to give up their privileges. They too claim that death has not yet occurred; that they still observe some tokens of life; and they too are opposed to a speedy interment. On the other hand, the health officers, reason and common sense, insist upon the necessity of the burial. They claim that the process of dissolution will infect the neighborhood with the germs of disease. Thus the defunct idea is finally buried, in spite of all remonstrances; and posterity either passes by its grave indifferently or places a wreath of evergreen upon it, as the case may be.

As there occur cases of death among men every day which, though unnoticed by the multitude, cast their gloom over the circles in which the departed had moved, thus ideas are dying away in and with almost every generation, the death of which affects only those who stood in near relationship to them. And thus have we, the Israelites of the present generation, been the witnesses of the death of an idea which was conceived more than two thousand years ago by our nation, which passed its childhood, manhood, and old age under its protection, and which has now expired after a long and marvellous career, never to be revived again.

The idea to which I refer is no other than the hope of our nation in the advent of a personal Messiah who would collect the scattered remnants of Israel under one banner, re-establish them in Palestine, rebuild Jerusalem in its former glory, and make Zion the capital not only of the Holy Land, but that of the whole world.

In the following lectures I shall give the eulogy of this idea, and trace its history from its very conception to the hour of its death. May it suffice, however, at present, if I explain the reasons first why I selected such a topic, and then why I maintain that the idea of the advent of a Messiah has died of late; is stone dead now, and ought to be buried by the side of similar defunct ideas, in spite of all opposition which may be raised against its final interment.

Although our nation is one of the oldest, if not the oldest, on earth; although it has lived on every continent, in every zone, in every climate; although we have a history, a literature of our own, excelled by no other; it has been our misfortune that we have never been understood by our neighbors. At best, we have been looked at with distrust; and though we have always thrown in our lot with our fellow-citizens in happiness and adversity, though we have been born and raised among them for generations, we have always been denounced by them as a foreign element, as a sect, the aspirations and hopes of which differed widely from those of the majority. This misunderstanding, this distrust, has not been removed even in our time and in this our country. You meet with it wherever you turn in political, social, mercantile, life. One of the reasons why we were and are distrusted is, as it appears to me, that we were and are still supposed to consider our country as only a temporary domicile, or, in other words, that we are suspected of indifference toward our country and its inhabitants. We are said to yearn for a return to the land of our forefathers, and to be impatiently awaiting the time when a Messiah shall appear among us, and not only restore our political independence, but make us the masters of the world. If this were the case, if these were indeed our hopes and aspirations, I must say that our neighbors would be perfectly justified in distrusting us; for I agree with them that a man cannot have two countries at the same time, that he can be attached with sincerity to only one country. The man will never be a good American citizen who always dreams of a return to the country from which he came, and who delights only in the customs and usages of the fatherland.

But in this regard our neighbors were and are entirely mistaken. Not one of us cares to leave this country except on a visit; not one of us harbors in his heart any love for Palestine, unless it is that esteem in which classical ground is held by every man of culture: there is not one among us who expects the advent of a Messiah.

I always took it for granted that, with the exception of the ignorant, our fellow-citizens were aware of the fact that modern Judaism has long since discarded the hope in the advent of a Messiah, and that the modern Israelite is with all his heart and soul a citizen of the country in which he lives, and where he is granted human rights; but how great has been my surprise when in conversation with persons of high culture, of eminent scholarship, and of rare intelligence, I have found that they still believe us yearning for Palestine and praying for the advent of a Messiah, that they still think it a distinguishing feature between Jews and Christians that we believe the Messiah will come, and they that he has come. Open the geographical text-books which your children use at school, and you will find therein, in cold print, the statement that the Jews are a sect which is expecting a Messiah, who, as the Christians claim, has already come; and thousands of children memorize this erroneous statement year after year, and hear it repeated Sunday after Sunday at church; and we do absolutely nothing to contradict it and to rectify the error. It is therefore time, high time, that we make an attempt to enlighten our fellow-citizens in regard to our hopes; that we show to them the tomb in which the Messianic expectations of our nation are buried.

But although the misunderstanding may be partly laid before our door, inasmuch as we may have neglected to notify the Christian world promptly of the demise of the Messianic idea, we shall find that our Christian friends are not entirely faultless; for they have never shown any readiness to accept our information: they have reasons for not believing in the death of that idea, and they remonstrate against its interment. The same people who distrust our patriotism on the ground that we are expecting a Messiah and wishing to return to Palestine,— these same people are shocked and horrified when we tell them that we do not any longer expect a Messiah, and have not the faintest desire for a political restoration of our people. Now why? Because such intelligence strikes at the root of their own religious belief. The whole structure of their religion rests upon the belief of the Jewish nation in the advent of a Messiah. As long as this idea has been strong and vigorous among us, their building has stood firm; but from the moment the idea expired, from the moment its fallacy was demonstrated, their structure could not be saved from its downfall. They are actually placed between the two horns of a dilemma, and do not know which to choose. They do not know at present whether they should prefer us to be indifferent citizens or to be indifferent to Messianic expectations. For this very reason, it becomes doubly our duty to spread that intelligence as far as our circles reach, and to show to the Gentile world that Messianic expectations are not essential to Judaism; that Judaism can exist without them; that the Jewish-mission is not chained to Palestine, but embraces the whole world; that, metaphorically speaking, Israel itself is the Messiah whom God has destined to enlighten the nations of the earth.

In the course of my subsequent lectures, I shall therefore show that the Messianic idea had originally a political, and by no means a religious or spiritual, tendency; that it never appeared as a manifestation of a healthy condition of the body politic of the Jewish people, but rather as a mental disease, as a mania, as an epidemic, which would break out at times of great national calamity. I shall show that these epidemics repeatedly occurred with greater or less force up to the eighteenth century. I shall show how the Messiah, originally political, was transformed by degrees into a divine messenger, directly descending from heaven, who should re-assemble, in a miraculous manner, the Israelites from all the corners of the earth, bring them to Palestine, raise the dead, judge the whole world, past and present, punish the wicked and reward the faithful, and establish a universal government and a universal religion. I shall show how the Messianic fancy finally pined away when the new era shed its full light upon its absurdities, until it died out entirely.

The word *Messiah* itself deserves a close scrutiny. The Hebrew word *mashach* means to spread an oily or greasy substance over a person or an article; but right from the start it implied a sacred ceremony. Jacob poured oil upon the stone upon which he had rested and enjoyed that wonderful dream. Moses is ordered to prepare oil for the special purpose of anointing his brother Aaron as high priest, and also to anoint the different articles of furniture which were to be used in the tabernacle, in order to give him and them a certain sanctity in the eyes of the people. The narrative and command are given in such a matter-of-fact way that there cannot be the least doubt that, among ancient nations, especially those with whom the Israelites had come in contact, there must have been in use a similar ceremony of installing the highest officials, kings or priests, into their exalted position. Why oil was poured over their heads, in what connection oil stood with the dignity of the office, what the meaning of the custom was originally, when and where it originated, is more than I can tell; and, I think, more than anybody else can tell. The fact, however, remains that the ceremony of pouring oil upon the head of a person meant to consecrate him for a high political position. The Mosaic constitution had provided for a hierarchical government. The high priest alone was, therefore, to be anointed. After the decline of the primitive priesthood, we find that Samuel anointed Saul, and afterward David, as kings over Israel; and that from that time it became necessary for a king to be anointed in order to be acknowledged by the people as their legitimate sovereign. Mashiach, or the anointed, is, therefore, synonymous with the word *king*. Whenever in political language that word has been made use of, it had no other meaning, and could have had no other, than that of legitimate king. None, however, of all the so-called Messiahs who have appeared in the course of history, has undergone or has found it necessary to undergo the ceremony of having oil poured over his head; which evidently shows that the original meaning having been forgotten or obliterated by that time, the word *mashiach*, or, in the Latin version, *messias*, denoted simply a king, but not a divine messenger.

The illustrious reign of David, and the independence which the united kingdom of Israel enjoyed during his government, appeared in the next centuries the more glorious the more the weakness and dependence of Israel were then felt. At a time when royalty was hereditary, and people not seldom waged war to install an infant upon a throne for no other cause than that it was the lineal descendant of a king, it was quite natural that when for the first time the hope of a regeneration of the Israelitish kingdom was expressed, a Messiah, or king, was expected, who, descending from David, should also be heir to his courage, power, and success, and should bring back the glory of the past.

All Messianic expectations centred, therefore, in the requirement of a lineal descent of the Messiah from the house of David. None of them, however, has ever proved his descent; and to-day such a proof has become entirely impossible, as all traces have been lost.

The absurdity of upholding the hope in the advent of a Messiah in our time or any future time, will furthermore appear in a still more glaring light if we take away its theoretical fanciful garment, and translate it into practical reality.

Supposing a person should appear among us who should be equipped with all the necessary testimonials of his divine mission, even of his lineal descent from David, if this could improve his title; supposing he should by some means gather the Israelites from all parts of the world and settle them again in Palestine, — would this enhance our happiness? Supposing, even, he should find for us room and employment in the new country, supposing all impossibilities should be made possible by him, let me ask the one question, What kind of a government do you think the Messiah would establish? The republican form would be entirely out of question. Just imagine a Messiah elected for a term of one, four, or seven years; just imagine a Messiah passing through the ordeal of a political campaign in which not only his own record, but that of his ancestors upward to David, should be exposed and laid bare to ridicule! No, those who expect a Messiah must give up forever the hope that he would establish a republican government. Would it be a constitutional monarchy? Equally absurd. Imagine a Messiah quarrelling with his parliament, and the latter refusing to vote the necessary appropriations! The only imaginable form of government under a Messiah would be despotism. Under his rule there would be no free thought, no free speech, and surely no free press. No opinion differing from that of the Messiah either in politics or religion would be tolerated, and should we call this happiness? Would this condition of slavery be the *ne plus ultra* of our hopes and aspirations? For this state of mental stagnation should we be supposed to pray? Absurd, thrice absurd.

At the time when the Jews were crowded into the Ghetto; at the time when our ancestors were denied the most fundamental of all human rights, namely, the right to live; at the time when they were chased from country to country, and had to purchase at heavy expense the privilege of breathing the foul air of their secluded quarters; at the time when ignorance ruled supreme among them, and still more among their oppressors; at such a time all fanciful hopes and fantastic expectations were permissible, and no picture of Messianic happiness could be overdrawn. Did they care what kind of government a Messiah would institute? Did they care for liberty of speech and freedom of the press? They would have kissed the feet of the most selfish despot, provided he would have granted them recognition, and placed them on an equal footing with their fellow citizens.

But we, the children of the nineteenth century; we, the free citizens of a free republican country; we, the graduates of the best schools the world has seen; we, whose hands have learned to fold and cast a ballot, we do care under what kind of government we are placed; we do love the privileges of a republic, and would not for the world change it for any other form; we do value free thought, free speech, and free press, as the highest attainments of humanity; and we shall never renounce them. How could we, therefore, be expected to yearn after Messianic despotism; how could we be suspected of infidelity to a country which grants us these boons, and of favoring Palestine, where all these glorious privileges would have no room?

The hope in the advent of a Messiah and in the restoration of Israel is surely dead. It has died out in the heart of every intelligent American Israelite. As with the increase of knowledge the horizon of the human mind has been widened, as the universe has grown larger for us than it ever was for bygone generations, as God even has grown infinitely larger, mightier, and holier than ever, thus our hopes have grown in proportion. They have lost their national character, and have become universal. We have given up all those fanciful notions of a political restoration of Israel through the instrumentality of a Messiah, and have adopted in their place the hope that all humanity will sometime reach by steady evolution a degree of happiness far beyond the present, and far beyond description; a state in which the evils still adhering to mankind will be removed, and its virtues increased and developed. United, and hand in hand with all our human brethren, we shall strive to advance toward this goal; and if there must be a distinction between us, let it be that of a generous competition as to who shall reach the mark first.

II.

"TWO THOUSAND YEARS AGO."

UPON what does the earth rest? This question greatly agitated the minds of people before the time of Newton and Copernicus. The answer was that it rests upon the back of an enormous elephant. But the inquisitiveness of human nature could not be set at rest so easily. Another question was raised: Upon what does the elephant rest? Answer: The elephant stands on top of an immense turtle. Yet this answer even did not give the desired satisfaction. The new question turned up: Upon what does the turtle rest? Instead of answering this time, the scientist of that age grumblingly complained in rather strong language that one fool would be likely to ask more questions than ten wise men could answer; and thus the conundrum was never solved.

Whenever we turn to historical research, we are in a similar quandary. We lack a basis which could safely carry our argument. We brag a great deal about historical knowledge and historical facts; but whenever we are called upon to bring them to light we find that our knowledge is very limited; that there are comparatively few real historical facts; and that our so-called history, with all our argumentation on top of it, floats, like that gigantic turtle, upon nothing.

Ancient history especially has mixed up a few grains of truth with such a bulk of fiction that it is now well nigh impossible to sift the wheat from the chaff. Some few scraps of statements made by some writer as the facts appeared to him individually,—for the most part not even corroborated by a contemporary,—have been handed down to us and palmed off on us as history. But even if we were ready and willing to accept the statements of a Herodotus, a Tacitus, a Livy, or a Josephus, as plain and absolute truth, with our best intentions we could not supply another deficiency; namely, that by the slow and laborious process of copying and recopying the manuscript by hand, in course of time so much of the original must have been changed, so many interpolations and additions must have been added to it, that if the original writer should be confronted to-day with his works, he would probably deny his authorship. And, after all, how did these writers know? History was never written at the time when the facts occurred. The current of the present is so swift and rapid, the multitude of facts taking place at every moment is so overwhelming, that the quickest camera could not take a correct negative of them. It is furthermore impossible for men to be both actors and spectators; we cannot be at the same time upon the stage and in front of it. History, therefore, has always been written by posterity. Now you will acknowledge that it would be a difficult task to-day to write a correct history of, let me say, the life of George Washington, although we are in possession of the archives containing all the official documents written or signed by him; although we have the files of the newspapers published at his time at our disposal, and many other advantages which the historian of former ages never had at his command. Tacitus, for example, had never seen Germany or Judea; still he wrote extensively about these countries. All his information was obtained from soldiers who had been there; and he took their yarns for facts: and we too have become accustomed to take them for facts. And this very Tacitus lived and wrote at a time when the Romans stood at the summit of civilization, and poets and writers were growing up among them like mushrooms.

In regard to Jewish history, and subsequently to that of the origin of Christianity, the entanglement is not less bewildering, although past generations have attempted to solve the difficulty and to find a desirable historical basis by cutting the Gordian knot in a somewhat peculiar way. They picked out a certain number of literary works relating their own history and that of their nearest neighbors, and attributed them to a divine authorship. They claimed that God himself had dictated, word for word, both the Old and the New Testament. From such divine statements there was of course no appeal. God, who knows the past as well as the future, could not err; he stood above all human criticism: and it was a long time before the Bible was submitted to a close historical scrutiny. For centuries, it has been a heresy, almost a crime, to doubt one iota of this sacred literature; to doubt that Moses wrote all the books attributed to him; to doubt that the Psalms were all written by David, or the Ecclesiastes by Solomon; to ask in what way and by what means the first correct copy of the orations of the prophets was obtained, or to consider these speeches as pertaining to their time only, or to the immediate future; and so on *ad infinitum*. For the so-called believer there was and is no appeal from the letter of scripture.

In my research after the origin of the Messianic idea, I shall, therefore, not argue with the believers. Modern Judaism does not believe blindly: it reasons. Although I take a just pride in the grand literature which our nation has brought forth and accumulated; although I maintain that all literature is inspired; that no man can write one single sentence unless he is divinely inspired; the books of the Bible are to me, as they are to every intelligent man to-day, products of human, and not of divine, authorship.

All the imperfections which adhere to human productions adhere also to the Bible. The men named as the authors of the different books were not their authors in reality. The real authors lived and wrote much later than the facts occurred which they describe. They collected their knowledge from tradition and hearsay; but though they wrote in good faith, and according to their best understanding, without the least desire to impose, their views must have been limited. Neither can they be held responsible for the changes in the text made by copyists and revisers during the hundreds of years which elapsed between them and the first authentic edition which is in the possession of our time. I shall, therefore, touch them but slightly; and I wish it understood, from the start, that the renowned eleventh chapter of Isaiah is nothing more to me than a beautiful picture, painted in Eastern colors, of that time of peace which the orator hoped humanity would sooner or later reach. If we were to picture that time to-day, we should probably give it a different coloring and a less picturesque perspective; but we should surely omit the fourteenth verse as in contradiction to the letter and the spirit of the whole previous oration, and as unbecoming to a true lover of peace.* With no other or better material at hand than scripture offers, I am, however, compelled to rest some of my arguments upon the turtle, and to let the turtle float wherever it pleases you.

The first traces of a hope in the advent of such a person as a Messiah are to be found not earlier than in the time shortly before, during, and shortly after, the Babylonian exile. The calamities which had befallen, first the house of Israel, and then the house of Judah, had so discouraged the Israelites that they despaired of their own ability to help themselves; and therefore they hoped for a miraculous interference of God in their behalf.

They yearned for the independence of the time of David, of which tradition must have brought to them the most glorious reports. A descendant of David was, therefore, to appear and win for them again the respect of their

---

* Isaiah 11:14. But they shall fly upon the shoulders of the Philistines toward the west. Together shall they spoil the children of the east; upon Edom and Moab shall they lay their hands; and the children of Ammon shall obey them.

neighbors, and make their voice heard again in the council of the nations.

There is nothing whatever that is unnatural or absurd in such a hope. Up to the last two decades, the Germans too were hoping for a restoration of the German Empire to its former mediæval glory. Hundreds of beautiful myths and legends predicted the return of the Kaiser Frederick I., or, as he was popularly nicknamed, Friedrich Barbarossa, "der Rothbart," who, as the legend ran, had never died, but was sleeping in the caves of the Kyffhäuser Mountain. With him a large army of valiant knights was said to be concealed in the subterranean abode, who would, at the proper season, awake and break forth under his leadership to liberate Germany and to restore its union. It was told that, after every lapse of a hundred years, the old emperor, whose beard had grown all around the marble table upon which his head was resting, would call a shepherd to his cave, and ask him whether the ravens were still flying around the mountain-top; and that upon his affirming the fact, he would sadly exclaim,

> "Und wenn die schwarzen Raben
> Noch fliegen immer dar,
> So muss ich nochmals schlafen
> Verzaubert hundert Jahr."

One of the first and signal deeds with which Barbarossa was expected to astonish the world was to wage a successful war against France. What should you think of it if, a thousand years hence, a historian should prove by these myths that the Germans had been expecting a Messiah, and that he actually appeared in the year 1862, but was called, not Barbarossa, but Bismarck?

The scraps of literature which we possess relating to the time before and after the Babylonian exile, and which seem to speak of a Messiah, are of about the same character and the same value as the legends of Barbarossa. They express the hope of a down-trodden nation in a restoration to former glory.

However, after the second Commonwealth had been firmly established, though by far different means than expected, after the second temple had been built, the Jews enjoyed a period of unprecedented prosperity. The yoke of the Persian Empire rested lightly upon them. They paid a small tribute; and as long as they paid it promptly, they remained unmolested. All Messianic expectations were therefore forgotten.

During this long season of prosperity, the original Mosaic doctrine maintaining the belief in one God came to full bloom; and idolatry, formerly flourishing among them, died away entirely. The laws collected and compiled by Ezra, and firmly planted by Nehemiah, fitted admirably to their condition. They were excellent laws, such as no other nation could boast of. The belief consequently grew up that they were of divine origin; and that as long as the nation should strictly adhere to them, it would be successful and prosperous; but that the slightest deviation from them would again bring the wrath of God upon the people, and that they should be exiled, as their ancestors had been before.

When the Persian Empire fell a prey to Alexander the Great, the condition of the Jews was not materially changed. It was of little importance to them to whom they paid their taxes, whether to the Persians, Egyptians, or Syrians. The closer intercourse with the Greeks tended in the beginning rather to broaden their own philosophy, and the Greeks, who had been accustomed to call all other nations barbarians, were, in their turn, greatly astonished to find such just laws, such deep philosophy, such high culture, in a nation of which they had scarcely heard before.

But by degrees some of the Jewish youth became attracted by Greek culture and customs. At that time the cultured classes of the Greeks were by no means gross idolaters. Socrates had not died in vain, nor had Plato and Aristotle lived in vain. The practices of Greek idolatry were at that period a mere consequence of indolence. Idolatry had become too absurd for the educated classes to attempt to wean the rest of the people from it. Their philosophers claimed that the lower classes were in need of some superstition, and advised to let well enough alone. When Hellenism and Judaism finally clashed against each other, the forcible introduction of Greek idols into Palestine was more a matter of policy with Antiochus than of sincerity. Though a few young men sided with the Greeks, the mass of the Jewish people were sincere in their attachment to God. By no means would they suffer the least idolatrous rite to be practised in their country; and the few who had been influenced by the Greeks, and had adopted with their customs also the indolence and indifference of that age towards religion, were decidedly in the minority. While the Hasmonean wars may appear as a religious warfare, well-informed historians claim that they were a political contest. Antiochus wished to form one large and well-cemented empire of all the small nations which were tributary to him, that he might be able to withstand the power of the Roman Republic, which, since the fall of Carthage and Corinth, had already spread its threatening shadows in an eastern direction. He thought it good policy to tie Judea to his domain by the bonds of the same superstition, as all religion was called by the philosophers of that age. But his policy was a mistaken one. Just here the Jews drew the line. He would have found them willing to pay any tribute whatsoever and to render military service; but they would not permit their religious autonomy to be touched. They flew to arms, and under the leadership of the noble Hasmonean family, a contest raging for several generations followed, which was carried on with changing luck on both sides. At the close of these wars, they found to their greatest surprise that they had gained more than they had ever expected. They had originally fought for home rule only: now they found themselves independent, their country enlarged, with a king,—a descendant not of David but of the Hasmonean house,—at their head. They did not know how to account for their good luck.

The people who had taken up arms for their God and their religion, and who had been called Chasidium, the pious, to distinguish them from the frivolous Hellenistic element, now split into two factions on account of it.

The greater part believed that their success was the result of their obedience to the laws of God; that God had, in fact, interfered in their behalf; and that therefore their mission was plain and self-evident. They must enforce the law most rigorously, and refrain from all intercourse with other nations, especially with the Greek. They were called Pharisees, Perushim, interpreters of the law; but they were conscientious, and by no means hypocrites. The other class had seen more of the world. It was composed of all those who not only had been the leaders in previous battles, but who had obtained as statesmen, by shrewd political wire-pulling, more than their swords could ever have won for them. They knew the secret of their success. Their good luck had been the result of Roman influence. That great and insatiable republic had stretched its hand nearer and nearer towards its prey. Divide and rule had been its motto. It had taken up quite disinterestedly, as it then appeared, the Jewish cause, as well as that of the other tributaries of which the Syrian kingdom was composed, and had assumed the rôle of a protector over them. Little did these small nations dream at that time that after the fall of Syria and Egypt their turn would come to be annexed to the Roman Empire.

The Sadducees, as they were called, who had been prominent in all the political manœuvrings, knew, therefore, too well that rigor and a blind belief in the help of God would not do; that they must yield to a compromise; or, in other words, that they must not totally ignore the present. This split in the formerly compact party accelerated, though it did not cause, the doom of the Jewish nation.

Indeed, their dream of independence and the lustre of the Hasmonean dynasty were of a short duration only. Judea became a Roman province before the inhabitants became aware of it; and, while the Roman senate left to them some shadow of self-government, it had already fastened the shackles to the victim. When the Jews came to themselves, they found themselves tied, hand and foot, in the power of an almighty foe. Their condition, indeed, was then most pitiable. Their independence was crushed, their king a mere puppet in the hands of the Roman Cæsars, their high priest without authority, their laws set at nought by the whims of the Roman proconsul. Roman legions fattened at the public expense: rapacious Roman procurators drained the resources of the land by heavy taxation.

Jerusalem had then three separate courts, which rivalled one another in luxury. There was the high priest and his household, and with him all the temple functionaries, who were supported in grand style by the reverence of the people and from fear that God would withdraw his protection from them unless every tax which was due to the temple were scrupulously paid. Next came the royal household, the dignity of which was to be upheld at a heavy expense.

Finally, there was the Roman governor, who knew perfectly well how to make a public office pay, and who imitated the extravagance of Rome. No wonder that times were hard for the tax-payer; no wonder that the peaceful real-estate owner grew riotous; no wonder that the burden became unbearable, and that the nation despaired of itself. At this period of national calamity, at the time when the days of the Jewish commonwealth were already numbered, the hope broke forth with new vigor that, as human efforts were of no avail, God himself would, must, interfere and set matters aright. The first commonwealth had fallen on account of the sins of their forefathers; but this time they were innocent: they had strictly obeyed the law; and God, if he were just, was in honor bound to come to their rescue. Neither was there any cause to doubt the ability of God to save them. Had he not returned the captives to the land of their forefathers? Had he not assisted their very parents and grandparents in their struggle against the power of Syria? There was not the least doubt in their minds that the present time was only a time of trial, and that God would soon rectify matters. During the Hasmonean era, the prophetical books had become quite popular. They were now read and re-read with eagerness, and were naturally interpreted to fit the present needs and hopes. The idea spread that, as the descendants of the Hasmonean house had not the courage to oppose the greed of rapacious Rome, they had forfeited their right to the throne; and that a scion of the house of David would therefore be sent by God, who should drive the Romans out of the country, and bring back the former independence and glory.

The maltreated, overtaxed farmer, the unemployed artisan, the bankrupt merchant, the demoralized soldier, the aristocrat who had to bend his head before the haughty Roman magistrate, — they all drank eagerly the hope of the advent of a Messiah, and awaited impatiently the favorable moment when, sword in hand, they could shake off the yoke of the oppressor; and they had not the least doubt that, at that auspicious moment, God would send the right man to lead them to success.

But there were also people who were not half so sanguine as their more zealous neighbors. They knew that a revolt against Rome would be useless. Rome could only take of him who owned property; and it was only for the improvement of the condition of the property-holder that war was to be undertaken. They sought, therefore, safety in a change of the whole social system. Nihilistic and communistic tendencies began to develop. These classes too were expecting the man who should have the power of establishing an ideal society after their heart; and who would, according to the peculiar language which they used, save the world.

The hope in the advent of a king duly anointed for his office, who would improve the state of affairs, grew stronger and mightier every day the more unbearable the national misery grew. It was again the natural growth of the unhealthy condition of the time; and the sicker the national body grew, the wider spread and the more intense grew the mania.

The Roman authorities on their part wished for nothing better than that a crisis should be reached as soon as possible; and they rather stimulated a revolt of the people, in order to obtain a pretext for crushing the nation at once. They, too, were wishing that the Messiah, with whose appearance they were threatened day by day, would come. They had nothing to lose, and all to win. And thus day by day added to the fuel, which, if fired by an over-zealous or uncautious hand would spread its conflagration over the land.

In vain did the cautious among the people raise their voice of warning; they could not undo what generations had prepared. Such was the condition of the time shortly before the destruction of the second temple; and the first flash of lightning which appeared and disappeared in the political sky of the second commonwealth, the appearance of Jesus of Nazareth, predicted the coming hurricane which swept the Jewish nation, politically, from the face of the earth.

III.

"THE CARPENTER'S SON."

IT is not without some hesitation nor without some embarrassment that I open the discussion of the life and mission of a man who, though he sprang from Jewish parentage, and is said to have lived the life of a conscientious Jew, has been placed between our race and the rest of civilized humanity as a barrier to exclude us from a more intimate intercourse with our fellow-men; whose very name still alienates from us to-day the affection of our fellow-citizens, though almost nineteen centuries have passed since its bearer walked the ground of Palestine. Neither must I lose sight of the veneration in which he is held by our Christian friends, many of whom love in him the ideal of a magnanimous, high-minded, and noble man; while millions of others still confide in him in life and in death, and adore and worship him as a God. It is, therefore, not more than simple courtesy on our part if we respect their feelings, as we wish our own respected, and if we discuss our subject with as much careful delicacy and tenderness as we can possibly grant to a historical research, which is intended not to obtain notoriety, but to instruct; to weed out existing prejudices, and to establish a better understanding between us. I beg you, therefore, to distinguish well between the ideal Jesus, who has been a creation of Christianity, and the historical Jesus of Nazareth as he lived and died.

You can imagine at any time, if you so choose, a human body in such giantlike proportions that its head should reach the zenith while its feet should touch the nadir. In the very same way, you may imagine all the qualities of the human soul raised to their highest degree of perfection. We Israelites are accustomed to attribute these qualities of the spirit in their highest perfection to an invisible God; to the One God who has created the universe, and supports and governs it in wisdom and love; while our Christian friends have become accustomed to affix these very same attributes to a human form, to that of Jesus of Nazareth. Herein we differ; and, therefore, I shall have nothing to say concerning the ideal structure which has been built up during the last nineteen centuries, which is in the process of building yet, and which will not be finished before humanity has reached the highest round on the ladder of civilization.

I beg also to differ historically in two other

points with our Christian friends; and I hope they will not consider my utterances as disrespectful. I maintain that Jesus was not the founder of Christianity; that he never planned it nor laid its foundation; but that his personality has been brought into the Church, and used as its corner-stone. I claim, furthermore, that there are no historical sources whatsoever from which we could derive authentic information concerning his life, his deeds, and his death. This point is of such grave importance that I must dwell on it, with your permission, a minute or two before I proceed one step further.

There are only three sources from which it has become customary to quote in regard to Jesus of Nazareth. The first and foremost of them is the New Testament. Again I must caution my hearers that I do not believe in a divine authorship of any book whatsoever, be it called the Old or the New Testament, and that I shall always refrain from arguing a historical point with a so-called believer. If one wishes to believe that Homer was divinely inspired, and that the Iliad and Odyssey were dictated to him by God himself, and that therefore these books must be true, word for word, I shall not object. Let him believe, then, that Cyclops Polyphemus had but one eye in his forehead, and that Ulysses blinded him; let him believe that the hero visited Hades, and conversed with his former friends; let him believe whatever he pleases. But when we come to discuss historical facts, we must be unhampered by belief. Bibliographers have long since proved that the Four Gospels, which, after all, contradict one another in important points, were written more than a century later than the death of Jesus; not by eye-witnesses, but by people who collected their material from tradition, and who had already a principle, a theory, to affirm by their story. I do not question at all their veracity or sincerity; but they lacked for their narrative the authentic material, and could not help being biassed in their judgment. These literary products lose still more in the eye of the critic by the fact that the original text has been tampered with since. Only of late, a scrap of parchment has been discovered which contains a passage from one of the Gospels. Scientists place its age as far back as the third and fourth century. In it an important passage, relating to the promised return of Jesus, is entirely omitted; which would prove, if it proves anything, that still later than the fourth century interpolations, if we shall not call them falsifications, of the original text, must have taken place. A jury which finds the testimony of a witness unreliable in one point generally throws out his testimony entirely; and so does the historian. To him the Gospels are of little historical value.

The second source is the historian Josephus, who lived at the time of Jesus, and consequently must have known of him, if the latter had, indeed, been a distinguished person or of any prominence. Though he gave considerable space to the narrative of minor events, Josephus originally never mentioned him. The celebrated and frequently quoted passage in his *Antiquities* (book xviii., chapter 3,) has been condemned by authorities, such as Nathaniel Lardner, as an interpolation; and Origen, the great Christian writer of the third century, shows by his writings *contra Celsum* that he did not know of that passage, which consequently must have been inserted much later and for a purpose.* Another historian, Justus of Tibe-

---

* I shall briefly give the arguments of Dr. Lardner, a very learned Presbyterian clergyman, who flourished in the early part of the last century. The passage reads thus:—

"At the time lived Jesus, a wise man, *if he may be called a man;* for he performed many wonderful works. He was a teacher of such men as received the truth with pleasure. He drew over to him many Jews and *Gentiles. This was the Christ;* and when Pilate, at the instigation of the chief men among us, had condemned him to the cross, they who before had conceived an affection for him did not cease to adore him. *For on the third day he appeared to them alive again; the divine Prophets having foretold these and many other wonderful things concerning him;* and the sect of Christians, so called from him, subsists to this time."

I have italicized the parts which Dr. Lardner criticised at length, occupying several pages (London edition, vol. vi., p. 487), but which I shall abridge. They are as follows:—

rias, lived at the same time; but not a word did he mention about the man who, according to the Gospels, must have created quite a stir.

1. This paragraph is not referred to by any Christian writer before Eusebius (in the fourth century), — the Greek fathers, such as Justin Martyr, Clement of Alexandria, Tertullian, and Origen, and the Latin fathers Minucius, Felix, Cyprian, Arrobius and Lactantius, nor by Chrysostom, a contemporary of Eusebius. These were all well acquainted with the writings of Josephus, and quote him in their works. Dr. L. says: "So extraordinary a testimony to our Saviour, in so celebrated a Jewish writer, should not have been unknown to them, if it had been in him."

2. This passage was wanting in copies of Josephus which were seen by Photius in the ninth century. The said writer in his Bibliotèque had no less than three articles concerning Josephus, and never notices such an important testimony; nay, more; Photius says: "This writer (Josephus), being a prejudiced Jew, makes not *even the least mention concerning him* (Christ) or the miracles done by him."

3. It interrupts the narrative; Josephus begins the chapter with a riot that took place in Jerusalem, in which a number of Jews were killed and wounded; then comes the paragraph above quoted, and next follows that another calamity befel the Jews. The reader will readily perceive that the paragraph which was stuck in between the first and second, or *another* calamity, is an interpolation; it is out of place.

4. If Josephus was a Jew, he admitted *too much;* and if a Christian, he said *too little* about Christ. I must add only one quotation — the idea would not strike an ordinary reader. He drew over to him many Jews and *Gentiles.* That is not true of the Lord Jesus, if intended of his own personal preaching; it was done indeed *afterward.* But this manner of speaking is more suitable to a writer of the second or third century than to Josephus.

Gibbon, in his Decline and Fall of the Roman Empire (Harper's ed., chap. 16, p. 298, in a note), says: "The passage

The third source is the Talmud; but here again we find an ominous silence concerning him. Not before the time that our ancestors were called upon to contest the religious structure which began to grow up upon him as its corner-stone, and to defend themselves against calumnious charges, is he mentioned, and then only slightly.

Besides these three sources, another argument is frequently brought into use in order to prove not only his existence, but his greatness. Behold, say our Christian friends, the marvellous growth of Christianity! See how it revolutionized the world, how it civilized the most barbarous nations! Could such a success have been achieved if its founder had not been a

concerning Jesus Christ which was inserted into the text of Josephus between the time of Origen and that of Eusebius may furnish an example of no vulgar forgery; and if any doubt still remains (here he refers to several writers who have proved it a falsity), it would appear pedantic were I to copy the names of eminent theologians who have written against or rejected the said passage; the proofs that it forms one of the numerous frauds which the Christians of the first three centuries deemed a virtue are overwhelming. The truth is, had Jesus really been the important personage represented, Josephus would doubtless have noticed him either as a God, a prophet, or an impostor; but as he mentions John the Baptist, and is utterly silent about Jesus, we may reasonably conclude either there was no such person, or that he was then deemed too insignificant, and that Josephus never heard about *the crucifixion or anything* concerning him."— *From an article of Jacob Norton, published in the American Israelite in April,* 1864.

man of great prominence, if he had not been able to impress his contemporaries with his mission to such an extent as was needed for the future success? Granted, they say, that there are no authentic literary evidences to be found concerning his life and deeds; is the mere existence of the Church not evidence enough for his greatness? Do not facts prove more than words?

This argument, however rational and reasonable it may appear, stands upon weak and tender feet. Indeed, if the plans for the Christian Church had emanated from him, if its doctrines had been promulgated by him, if its system had been suggested by him, then we could conclude from the work about its creator. But, even according to Christian sources, nobody dreamed less of such a structure than its supposed originator. Christianity was not his work; it was the product of peculiar circumstances, which all worked together in such a marvellous manner that we cannot fail to see the finger of God in its origin and development. The downfall of Hellenistic idolatry, which had been prepared by Greek philosophy long before; the extinction of the Roman Republic and the decline of the Roman Empire; the great migration of nations, which, issuing from the north, took a southward course, and changed the geography of the world; the death of antique civilization in the waves of barbarism, which, like a second flood, burst upon it, and covered the whole world for a considerable length of time,—all these circumstances together produced what to-day is called Christianity. Nothing can live in this sublunary world unless it is marked for life by God Almighty. Nothing succeeds unless God has destined it for success; and thus has Christianity a place on this earth and a mission to fulfil as well as Judaism. And in the course of my lectures I shall with pleasure give due acknowledgment to the great work which Christianity has indeed performed.

Taking it all in all, what may we reasonably presume about Jesus of Nazareth, the so-called Messiah? Although volumes have been written concerning his life and deeds, his whole history could be inscribed almost upon the nail of a thumb.

Jeshu, an abbreviation of Joshua, and Latinized into Jesus, was born of humble parentage. He was the son of Joseph, a poor carpenter, and Miriam, his wife, who were also the parents of several other children. It matters little to the historian that millions of people still ascribe to him a divine origin, and believe him the offspring of an immaculate conception. There are many more millions of people who believe to-day the very same story, but apply it to another man, to Buddha. Not only are such statements unhistorical, but I dare say that the passages in the Gospels relating to them were never written by a Jewish author: they were the products of a Grecian pen. The Greeks believed in the intercourse of their gods with mortal women, and saw no disgrace in such an adultery. All their heroes were demi-gods. Even Alexander the Great attempted to insinuate that Philip was not his real father, and that he was the son of a god. Greek vanity cared little that the chastity of their women was questioned whenever the customary compliment was rendered to a man by calling him the son of a god. The Greek and Roman populace would have never believed in Jesus the man, the reformer, the martyr, or the Messiah; but it was easy for them to accept him as the son of the Jewish God, Jehovah. The Jews, on the contrary, held the chastity of their women in so high a respect that they would not permit even a god to violate it.

About his childhood and early education nothing is known. He is said to have learned the trade of his father, that of a carpenter. Grown up to the age of manhood, he joined the sect of the Essenes, which was mostly composed of artisans, and represented the socialistic and nihilistic element of which I have spoken in my last lecture. They despised all earthly possessions, would not hold property, lived together in small bands, sharing everything in common. They would not marry: they believed that a change for the better could be effected only by an ascetic life, and that the Messiah whom every Jew was expecting at that time would transform the whole world into one large communistic brotherhood, in which there should be neither rich nor poor, and from which all the passions adhering to mankind should be removed. He may have grown into prominence in the rural districts where he sojourned. He may have spoken of the change which he expected to come over the world, with such a sincerity that, as is quite natural, his friends expected him to produce the change, and may have looked at him as the Messiah. Let me state right here that the name Messiah, or, as it is in Hebrew, Mashiach, is a misnomer, if applied to him; for he never was anointed for his mission by any authority whatsoever, real or fictitious. How can, therefore, a man be called Mashiach, the Anointed, the Christ, if he never was anointed? Even Christian sources do not claim that the act of anointment was ever performed on him.

Finally, perhaps he learned to believe in himself. A great many people do believe in themselves without being conceited. There would be no heroism if the hero did not believe in his own ability to perform the heroic deed.

Young men especially are apt to carry such a belief to an extreme; and he was a young man. At the time of his death, he was not older than thirty-three years; the most dangerous period of life, in which the young man attempts to transform his airy ideals into tangible facts.

The most critical season of the year was, at that time, the Passover Festival; a festival celebrated in remembrance of the liberation of Israel from Egyptian bondage. Every male person was bound to be present in Jerusalem during the seven days of this festival; and the spirit of liberty ran higher then than usual. The Roman procurator found it, therefore, always necessary to be present in person in the city, in order to quell any disturbance which was likely to arise, and to nip every revolt in the bud. You will perhaps understand much better the danger which the return of every Passover Festival brought to the front, if you place yourselves for one moment in the condition of that time.

Supposing our cherished Republic should have been changed into a despotic government; supposing some other nation stronger than we should defeat us in battle, and should keep us in a state of servitude; supposing that the indignation of the American people should watch for an opportune moment to break the chains of such a slavery; would not the Fourth of July then become the most critical and dangerous of all the days of the year? The remembrance of the glorious day when the heroic fathers of the country declared their independence would invite emulation. Any orator of mediocrity even could on that day stir up the people to riot and bloodshed.

The representative of the government then in power would, as a matter of course, be watchful of every movement, and have his soldiers in readiness to quell any disturbance. He would be at his post of duty on that day from morning till night, and feel relieved only when the last hour of that dangerous day had passed and the last fire-cracker had been set off.

In a similar plight was the Roman governor during the feast of Passover. His troops were stationed with great skill at the most important posts, and the garrison of Jerusalem re-enforced: police in uniform and detectives in disguise probably patrolled the streets, and reported promptly at headquarters. It may easily have happened when Jesus entered Jerusalem a few days before the festival that he was recognized and cheered by his rural friends: it is probable that the rumor spread among the people, which was ready for a revolt, that a Messiah had appeared, and would give the signal at the opportune moment: it is more than probable that this rumor reached the Roman authorities after it had been magnified to a large extent. The natural consequence was that Jesus was watched with suspicion; that every one of his steps was carefully guarded, and that just before the festival he was taken captive. Pontius Pilatus risked a *coup de main*. If Jesus was the Messiah indeed, his prompt imprisonment and execution would either intimidate the people and suppress the outbreak of a riot for some years, or it would make the people rise in arms at once, and hasten the crisis. Either way pleased the haughty Roman much better than the suspense in which he now was kept all the time.

His calculation was as correct as it was shrewd; but he was mistaken, nevertheless. The people would have risen in revolt if the great mass had considered the Galilean the right man to liberate them. But they expected a warrior, not a man of peaceful disposition: they expected a man of arms, and not a theorist. Neither was he an offspring of the house of David. The masses remained cold and indifferent when they heard of his arrest; and even the few friends of the unhappy Messiah deserted him in the hour of trial.

There is no evidence that he ever was tried before a Jewish tribunal, for the right of capital punishment had been usurped by the Romans long before; and even if there had been such a trial, he must have been acquitted, because the sympathies of his fellow-citizens would have been with him. But he was not tried or convicted by a regular Jewish court, as, on account of the holy day, there was no session. He was simply judged and convicted by the Roman authorities on the charge of conspiring against the Roman government; and he was executed in great haste the very next day, at a time when the assembled people witnessed the grand passover ceremonial in the temple. The mode of crucifixion was a Roman mode of execution; and the inscription *Jesus Nazaraeus, Rex Judaeorum*, Jesus of Nazareth, King of the Jews, which is said to have been affixed to his cross, was to show the charge which had been made against him.

Now this is a point upon which I must dwell a few moments longer. The malicious charge that the Jewish people, nineteen hundred years ago, tried, convicted, and executed an innocent man, has brought upon us indescribable misery, and bears even to-day its bitter fruit. This charge has been the cause of wholesale murder; and for nineteen centuries has our nation been persecuted for no other offence than that their ancestors had crucified Jesus. We were, and are still, called deicides, or, as vulgar language expresses it, Christ-killers. Absurd as it is to hold us responsible for an act committed by our ancestors nineteen hundred years ago, as ridiculous would it be for us to try to find an excuse for it. Granted that our ancestors were, in fact, the cause of his premature death, there is no excuse needed; for as long as capital punishment is not abolished, and circumstantial evidence is used to convict a criminal, or as long as political offences are punished with death, so long will cases of judicial murder never be avoided.

But the charge is as false as it is malicious. Scan the Jewish law from its beginning to its end and you will not find that such a trial as related in the Gospels could have taken place. The whole form of the proceeding as told in the Gospels is illegal according to the forms minutely described by the Jewish law. It shows again that the writers of the Gospels were not Jews, but must have been Greeks or Romans, who were ignorant of the Jewish law. And so it was; and with this fact the whole charge collapses. The whole charge was a fabrication of the early Church. At the time when the Gospels were written, most of the members of the Church were Gentiles; and it was at that time already evident that the Gentile world, and not the limited Jewish circle, was to be the future field for the missionary efforts of the Church.

How could a missionary approach a Roman

and tell him that his people had put to death the Son of God, their Saviour? Such a statement would have alienated the whole world from them; for the Roman Empire comprised almost the whole of the known world, and every individual took a certain pride in being a Roman citizen. The Jews, on the other hand, were only a small nation. They were then living in small communities scattered over all the provinces of the Roman Empire. They were furthermore disliked on account of their rigorous laws, which would not allow their amalgamation with their neighbors. They were hated at the imperial court on account of their obstinacy and the riotous character which they showed in frequent revolts. The charge was therefore laid before their door; and the Roman was told that the Jews had killed his Saviour; that the Roman authorities even had endeavored to save him from the violence of the populace, but had been unsuccessful. Such a story was pleasing to the Gentile world, and to a Roman it seemed both probable and plausible. The masses, which gained by it a pretext for venting their anger on a class which they hated, did not investigate the matter any further; and thus the unfounded and malicious charge, was handed down from generation to generation to this very day. Is it not high time that our liberal age and our enlightened fellow-citizens should finally drop that malicious charge, which, even if it were not a fabrication, could not reflect upon us? Is it not high time that bigotry and fanaticism should be silenced, and that the rising generations should be instructed to take those legends for what they are worth? It is not the Jew who is disgraced when the epithet of deicide or Christ-killer is hurled at him: it is the one who uses it; because this very expression gives unmistakable evidence, not only of his bigotry, his intolerance, and of his bad breeding, but of his ignorance; and, not for our own sake, but for his sake, I stand here and appeal to you to spread enlightenment wherever you can in regard to such an important matter.

IV.

JUDAISM THE MOTHER, AND CHRISTIANITY THE DAUGHTER.

THE time when Christianity was born was as peculiar and as remarkable in regard to religious matters as is perhaps our own present age. Then, as to-day, the educated classes, the pioneers of civilization, were ready for a change of front. Old ideas had outlived their usefulness, and the new ones had not yet developed far enough to take their places. The minds of the best and most conscientious men were therefore kept in a constant tension. The old pagan gods had lost their reputation, and the world was yearning for a God who should fill the void in the human heart. Though the most magnificent temples were erected at that period, there was an utter lack of true religious sentiment, and hypocrisy ran high. The splendor of the temples and the very attractions which the priests were compelled to offer, were unmistakable evidence that rites and ceremonies had lost their meaning, and with it their influence upon the worshipper. At that time, the eye of the pagan world instinctively turned toward the Jews. Their theology was pure, their doctrines founded upon philosophy, their laws just and comprehensive, their rites elevating and soul-inspiring, their ethics unsurpassed. Their intercourse with Greeks and Romans had introduced them to the world. They had multiplied, and were to be found everywhere. There were as that time more Israelites outside of Palestine than within. Large colonies of Jews were to be found in Persia and along the whole coast of Asia Minor: they had settlements in Greece, in Spain, in Gaul, in Italy, and especially in Rome. In Egypt they were almost the masters. They were the leading statesmen: they commanded the armies: they were the magnates of commerce and the owners of factories. In Leontopolis they owned a temple which rivalled in beauty and elegance that of Jerusalem. In Alexandria they had a number of synagogues, the most prominent of which is reported to have been of such dimensions that the loudest voice could not be heard from end to end, and that therefore a flag was waved from an elevated stand whenever the congregation was requested to rise and to join in the Amen. But what is of still greater importance, the Pentateuch had been translated into the Greek language. The Septuaginta, as this translation was called, had become a standard work; and all men of intelligence and learning had become familiar with it. No wonder, therefore, that Gentiles in large numbers embraced Judaism. From the interior of Asia a princess came with all her family to be initiated into the Jewish religion.

It is said, and it is well said, that every man has once in his life an opportune moment when he can make his fortune, but that only very few take hold of it, while the rest let it slip from their grasp. The same holds good for nations. That very period was the time when Judaism could have conquered the world. It would be an idle play of imagination for us to conjecture what our present condition would have been if our ancestors had made proper and prompt use of their opportunity. Alas, they did not. Perhaps an all-wise Providence had destined it for good reasons that they should not. There were two obstacles which then hindered the spreading of Judaism. In the first place, its customs were too rigorous. The Gentiles, though they acknowledged the correctness of Jewish theology and the purity of its ethics, were unwilling to submit to the Abrahamitic rite, to the table laws, and to the minute prescriptions concerning cleanliness. Judaism, on its part, was not ready to compromise with them, because, and this was the second obstacle, it was too aristocratic. Its doctrines maintained that the Israelites were a people chosen by God;

that the much admired laws were given to them for their own welfare; and that it was obligatory for them to guard, but not to spread them. Judaism, of course, would not reject the stranger who would knock at its doors; it would accept him cheerfully, provided he would take upon himself the whole burden of the law without any haggling; but it would not proselyte; it would not go and coax or force the stranger to come in. If these two obstacles could have been removed, the mastery of the world would have fallen as a consequence into the lap of Judaism.

There was one man living at that time who saw the golden apple hanging within such easy reach; he stretched forth his arm and broke it, but, alas, not for his own nation. It was Saul of Tarsus, better known as Paul. To him owes Christianity its life.

Paul was no rabbi. He was no scholar whatsoever, nor was he versed in Jewish literature. He knew the Bible in its Greek version only; he would misquote, in his letters to the Corinthians, a passage in Isaiah as occurring in the Pentateuch; but for all his ignorance in letters, he was zealous and practical.

Observing that Judaism could not and that it would not allow one letter of the law to be changed, he embraced with eagerness the legends of the crucified Jesus, which must have reached him in an exaggerated form; and, without having ever known him, he made him the corner-stone of the building which he proposed to erect. There was an old saying that the Messiah would do away with the law, as he would naturally usurp the power of issuing new orders. Paul made use of it, and accepted Jesus as the Messiah, no matter whether he had fulfilled what was expected of a Messiah or not. It was sufficient for him that a Messiah had appeared; for this gave him a handle to change or to abolish as much of the law as he, Paul, saw fit. With one stroke of the pen, as we should say, he removed one of the obstacles: he admitted Gentiles into Judaism without the performance of the Abrahamitic rite, and allowed them to eat whatever they pleased. Denounced by his Jewish brethren as a law-breaker, and distrusted even by the personal friends of the unfortunate Galilean, who were shocked to hear the words of their master interpreted by a stranger in such a peculiar way, Paul sought and found his friends among Gentiles. Supplying a long-felt want, his career became a success in spite of all the obstacles which beset his way. He was the first missionary whom the world has seen. Christian congregations grew up under the very print which his foot left upon the ground.

With him the Messianic idea, formerly local, took a universal turn. The Messiah now ceased to be an anointed king, expected to remove the political misery of the Jewish nation. He grew into a divine messenger, a son of God, sent from heaven to earth to save all mankind from the effect of sin. Though having been put to death, he would soon return, and hold stern judgment over the world. His friends would be royally rewarded, his enemies unmercifully punished. Thus the Messianic idea became a necessity for the Paulinian Church. Without it, it lacked all authority for the inroads made upon the law, the grandeur of which still remained the centre of attraction to the pagan world.

It would take years should I attempt to trace in weekly lectures the rise and growth of Christianity. May it suffice that I show to you its source, and that I establish the fact that it was built by Paul from sheer necessity, upon a mistaken interpretation of the Messianic idea, with which it stands and falls.

In the meantime, the Jews witnessed the appearance of another Messiah. His name was Theudas. He shared the fate of Jesus. Fadus, the Roman governor, caught him and his band, and beheaded him. Pilate did exactly the same which Fadus did a few years later; but nobody would claim to-day that the Jews tried and sentenced Theudas: nobody would hold them responsible for his death. Theudas, however, must have gained more notoriety than Jesus ever did at his time; for Josephus granted him a considerable space in his history.

When finally the cup of misery was full to the brim, and no help came from outside, the people arose in arms. A short but fierce struggle followed. Titus and his legions stormed Jerusalem, laid the temple in ashes; and with the destruction of Jerusalem Israel was stricken forever from the list of nations.

The seed planted by Paul had in the meantime grown up, and kept on growing. Christianity spread from day to day; and the daughter soon severed all connections with her mother. She went her own way; for she had a mission of her own to fulfil; a mission which neither Judaism nor Hellenism could have fulfilled with success: she had to civilize a world of barbarians. Judaism would have failed on account of its rigor: Hellenism, on account of its selfishness. Greek philosophy cared little for the welfare of mankind as a species: its attempts were directed toward individual happiness. But it forgot that individual happiness and national happiness stand in a mutual relation to each other, and that the one is impossible without the other. Whenever it failed to secure individual happiness, it was at a loss to account for it, and advised to escape the miseries of life by suicide. This was its last and only remedy. Nature, however, abhors destruction: neither the Epicurean nor the Stoic schools could ever win the favor of the masses. A Greek philosopher would have ridiculed it as absurd to stoop down to a slave or a barbarian, in order to educate him to higher and better principles. Not so Christianity. From her mother she had inherited the principles of freedom and equality; the principle of one God and one human brotherhood. From her she had learned the maxim, Love thy neighbor as thyself. Equipped with these gems from her mother's treasury, adorned with the ten sparkling diamonds of the Sinaitic law, she entered upon her path. What we should call to elevate or civilize was called by her to save; and to save the world she was bound. Let us give honor where honor is due. With unexcelled heroism, the disciple of the early Church would seek strange countries, savage nations, always carrying his life in his hands. He would fearlessly enter the cabin of barbarians, suffer their scorn, their anger, even death from their hands. He would never flinch nor shirk his duty. And such heroism overawed the barbarian: he submitted, and bowed before the new God.

There is a steel engraving, to be found in almost every large picture store, representing the following scene: Two savage-looking gladiators are seen fighting in the Circus Maximus of Rome, for the amusement of the masses. One has succeeded in throwing the net over his opponent, and in forcing him to the ground. His eyes beam with passion: he craves the blood of his victim. Uplifted in his sinewy arm, he holds the trident, a fearful weapon, wherewith to deal the deadly blow; when, lo and behold! a disciple of the early Church fearlessly places himself between the victor and his victim, with the cry, "Thou shalt not kill!" I do not know whether it is the skill of the artist or the subject chosen by him which produces the effect; but I can never pass this picture without emotion. Though the artist only imagined that scene, he took it, nevertheless, from life. Such scenes have occurred, not once, but a thousand times, until the brute in man was tamed, and the barbarian had learned, not only the lesson, "Thou shalt not kill," but the still greater one, "Love thy neighbor as thyself."

Christianity at the same time was accommodating itself to the pagan world. It did not ask for more than it could possibly get at a time. It granted indulgences, provided some of its lessons were accepted in exchange; and thus, step by step, it went further and further, until it had subdued the world; until it had civilized Germans, Goths, Celts, Huns, Mon gols, and all; until princes would yield to the frown of a bishop and warriors sheathe or unsheathe their swords at the command of the ecclesiastical head. Every unprejudiced man must acknowledge it, and I acknowledge it with pleasure, that Christianity has performed some remarkable deeds. It has abolished slavery, it has established monogamy, it has mitigated the evils of war, and by all means raised the standard of civilization.

But there is nothing obtained in this world without compensation. What is won on the one side is generally lost on the other. Christianity had stooped down to the pagan world to save it, it had yielded to its whims; but in its embraces it had lost its identity, and had become paganized in its turn. Step by step, it was dragged, let me say involuntarily, from its path. The Messiah was changed into a son of God, and the son soon unthroned the father. A mysterious trinity replaced monotheism: superstitious idolatry raised again its head. Upon the pedestals from which the early Church had thrown the jolly crowd of Greek gods and goddesses, the later Church erected the images of their saints. A Saint Martin took the place of Mars, the god of war; a Madonna, the place of a Minerva; a Magdalene, the place of a Venus. The churches were again desecrated into wonder-working institutions: the Christian priest assumed the splendor of his predecessor, and dressed in gorgeous style: the bishop of Rome became the heir of the late Pontifex Maximus. Reason was banished, and unbridled imagination was permitted to run riot. Paganism, it is true, had been Christianized; but during the process Christianity had become paganized. The world would surely have fallen back into its former barbarism, as the dreary Middle Ages indicated, if it had not been for Judaism. Yes, indeed: if it had not been for Judaism; and this is a fact which only few seem to know. Though bleeding from many a wound, though despised and maltreated by her haughty daughter, Judaism the mother still lived; and as long as she lived, she was a living protest against the frivolous conduct of her daughter. Her rigor, which had made her lose the command over a world, had protected her, on the other hand, from the dangerous embraces of paganism. She had preserved the purity of her doctrines, and still clung to reason in preference to blind belief.

At this juncture, it appears necessary to me to say a few words about *belief*, now we hear so much about believers and unbelievers, or infidels. Belief is always resorted to to offset reason; and a great many maintain that religion cannot be severed from belief. There are perhaps many Israelites who do not know it, and therefore will be scared when I tell them that Judaism is not built upon belief, but that it stands upon the firm rock of reason. You will never find in Jewish literature the command, "Thou shalt believe." This word was introduced into the religious vocabulary by Christianity. The mere belief in the Saviour was to save from eternal damnation. Standing upon a basis which could not withstand the pressure of reason, it was to be supported by beliefs. To believe did not mean to accept a statement as true because it could reasonably be expected to be true. No : to believe meant to accept a statement as true, although reason revolted against it. Only then the saving qualities of belief would come into play. There was, for instance, no merit in the belief in a God whose existence, though not perceivable by human senses, still stands to reason; but the belief that three are one and one three, a doctrine against which reason revolts, such a belief was soul-saving and meritorious. Let me give you another example. To believe that the sacred Scriptures were written in the same way as all other books, which they may surpass in diction and beauty, by human writers inspired for their work, or to believe that the soul of every writer, inventor, or discoverer, stands in a certain relation to the source from which all talent and genius spring and our spirits flow, such a belief, which stands to reason, was of no merit: it was, and is still, called unbelief. But to believe that God selected a certain man, and dictated him, word for word, an oration which he was to deliver, or a narrative which he was to write, assuming the responsible editorship himself, and using the man only as an amanuensis, such a belief, against which reason reasonably rebels, such a belief is still to-day demanded. The passage in which a Church Father says, *Credo, quia absurdum est,* "I believe, because it is absurd," was by no means intended as a sarcasm: it was the only standpoint of the Church. Whatever is reasonable needs not to be believed; it convinces; and the great God who has granted us the heavenly light of reason can not, does not, want us to exchange it for the dim lamp of blind belief. A religion which cannot stand the test of reason cannot endure forever: belief is a weak prop only, which sooner or later must break.

Christianity, because it could never prove its premises, was forced to cling to belief. Judaism, on the contrary, was not and is not under such a pressure. It accepts facts which have occurred in the past as true, as long as they are not unreasonable or proven to be unhistorical by new developments; and no merit is claimed for it nor any reward expected for it. This grants us full liberty of conscience.

At every critical period in the development of the Christian Church, Judaism, the mother, raised her voice of warning, and this voice was not to be silenced. Neither the sword of persecution nor the pyre and torture of the inquisition, not even ridicule, could chase away the maternal ghost, which would step between the daughter and her seducer at the critical moment. And thus the tide turned. Slowly but surely the daughter retraced her steps. Protestantism was the first step toward home. Judaism had so long protested against image-worship that the very best Christians began to listen, then to think: finally to join in the protest. Christian scholars secretly visited in disguise the learned men of Judah. They visited their miserable abodes, to be introduced by them to the mysteries of the Talmud, and to read with them the Bible in the original.* Here they drank in full draughts from the waters of life; and when Luther nailed his theses to the church door of Wittenberg, his hammer sounded the death-knell to idolatry. Four hundred years of retracing her steps are not a long time in comparison with the fifteen hundred years during which the Church was built; and considerable work has been done already We have arrived at that stage where the dogma of a trinity has been abandoned, and a Unitarian platform is erected in its place. Jesus of Naza-

* Reuchlin, Sebastian Munster, Egidio de Viterbo, and others.

reth, five hundred years ago the principal and foremost feature of the trinity, is now to our enlightened Unitarian friends not more than the ideal of a man; and I doubt whether the remaining eleven hundred will be consumed before he will not be more and not less than the carpenter's son. Hereditary sin, atonement through Christ, heaven and purgatory, eternal bliss and eternal damnation, all these superstitious doctrines have already fallen; and the sun of reason breaks through the clouds, and sheds its bright rays to-day over a world happier and better than ever before.

Has Judaism remained unchanged during all these centuries? In its principles, yes; in its forms, no. The principle that there is but one God, and none besides him, and the ten commandments, which are the necessary consequence of it, have remained unchanged, and will remain unchanged forever, until the whole human race shall have adopted them. They have already adopted them in theory, but not yet in practice. But in regard to forms we have changed. Thank God, we have advanced. The Jew of to-day is no longer the Jew of nineteen hundred years ago. We are no mummies: we are alive and wide awake to the demands of our time. We have learned a good many things: and I praise God for it that we have also forgotten a good many. The advancing

Israelite and the advanced, or, as I shall name him more properly, the returning, Christian stand to-day almost upon the same level. There are only two slight difficulties to be overcome; one on the part of our Unitarian friends, the other on both sides. The first is that our friends must give up the ideal embellishments with which Jesus of Nazareth is glorified, and reduce him to that place which he may have really filled. I know it: it will take some time before they shall overcome this difficulty; for it is not so easy as you may think to give up ideals to which you have become attached from your earliest childhood; nor must we forget that then they would lose their claim to the Christian name, so highly cherished by them. The other difficulty to be overcome by both sides is race prejudice. With the spread of intelligence, with a better understanding between both races, and with good will on both sides, I am almost certain that in course of time this difficulty too will be removed.

Mother and daughter, who even then will touch one another with the tips of their fingers only, will feel the magnetic current of love pass through their bodies. Nearer and nearer they will be drawn to each other, until at last, after a thousand years, they will be reunited in one loving embrace.

V.

A GENUINE MESSIAH.

MEN and events are seldom weighed by us in the scales of justice. It is the successful who generally carries off the admiration and appreciation of the world; and the popular adage says therefore correctly, Nothing succeeds like success. Success, however, is a product composed of two factors; the one of which is our own ability and ambition, the other an indescribable something, commonly called luck. The one is within ourselves, the other outside of us. We have full control over the first one, but no command whatsoever over the second. Nor are these two factors equal in value. The product *success* is obtained in some cases by the multiplication of great ability with a small quantity of luck; in others, by the multiplication of little ability with a great amount of luck. No success whatsoever can be reached if one of these two factors is lacking. The most talented, the most enthusiastic, will fail in his enterprise if luck does not favor him; and the choicest luck cannot tower up to the goal of success if not supported by some intelligence.

But, sad as the fact is, mankind never goes behind the returns. It never takes the time to examine the factors: it looks at the product only. If a man is successful, it bows before him in admiration: if his undertaking has been unsuccessful, it turns from him with disgust; at best with pity. A people arising to break the fetters which either a foreign nation or the party in power has tied around its limbs has always been a grand sight; and the attention of the world has always been directed toward the place where such an uprising has occurred; but it has always been the final success which has influenced the verdict. Whenever a nation has succeeded in liberating itself, the preceding struggle has been called a revolution: if it has failed in its enterprise, it has been called a rebellion. In the first case, the national leaders have been worshipped as heroes, and their praises have been sung by the poets of their time; in the other, they have been stigmatized as traitors, as ringleaders, as rebels; and though they may have sealed their love for their country with their blood, either gloriously on the battle-field, or ignominiously upon the scaffold, not a word has been said in their favor: not a pen has been stirred to transmit their name to posterity. At best, they have been defended; at best, some friendly hand has attempted to wipe away the stains with which their misfortune or ill luck has bespattered them.

My argument will appear with greater distinctness by the following comparison. Supposing the United States of America had been unsuccessful in their struggle against Great Britain, do you think we should look at the event as we do now? You may rest assured that the glorious time of a hundred years ago would be branded to-day as a time of rebellion; that the children at school would be instructed to detest the rebels, Washington and Franklin, and to glory in the patriotism of Arnold. They would not be told to memorize Longfellow's beautiful poem of the midnight ride of Paul Revere; and "God save the Queen" would fill the place of the "Starspangled Banner" in the singing-books of our schools. How many of us would take the trouble to examine the motives, the heroism, and the enthusiasm, of the noble men of '76? Few; for we all should silently acquiesce in the verdict of the world; or, as you may call it, in the verdict of history, which, after all, would have been influenced, not by the merit, but by the success of the cause.

Will humanity ever outgrow such injustice? I have good reason to believe that the historians of the future will adopt a more just measurement of men and events; that they will overhaul the whole building which history so far has erected, and that they will mete out justice unbiassed by the success with which an event had been accompanied; and I should advise you, my friends, whenever you go into historical research, to leave a wide margin in favor of the unsuccessful party.

I shall now acquaint you with such a party, and with a man who, if he had been successful, would have filled the world with his renown. He possessed the one factor of success, genius, talent, enthusiasm; but, alas, he lacked the other. Luck went against him. I shall conjure up before you the spirit of a man whom nobody to-day seems to know, but who, nevertheless, at his time had made a Roman emperor tremble upon his throne; whose very name spread terror upon Roman soil similar to that which, hundreds of years before, the name of Brennus and Hannibal had caused. Would that I could show you the last Jewish warrior in his full glory! Would that I could sing in loud strains the praise of the last Jewish hero, who, if ever a man has deserved the title Messiah, was worthy of it! If ever Messianic expectations have been realized, they were realized in Bar Kochba. He was, barring anointment, a Messiah who tallied, every inch of him, with the hopes which his nation harbored concerning such a man.

The Jewish nation has been and is still blamed for rejecting Jesus of Nazareth as a Messiah. They have been called a stubborn people, who would always maltreat its benefactors and best friends. False, thrice false! The Jews were, as they are still, wide-awake, and knew well how to distinguish a chimera from a reality. While they remained indifferent to idealistic dreamers, as Jesus and Theudas may have been, they arose as one man when the person appeared who had all the qualifications of a Messiah. They placed at Bar Kochba's disposal an army of not less than half a million of well-equipped soldiers. They heeded strictly his orders. There was not the least discord in their ranks; and during five years more than two millions of Jews sacrificed their lives for him and his cause. Does such devotion indicate blindness or stubbornness? Alas! Bar Kochba was not successful: his cause did not triumph. The hero was therefore degraded to a rebel, and the last glorious struggle of our nation was stigmatized as a rebellion.

Jerusalem had fallen in the year 70 of the new era, and Judea had been made a Roman province. Years of misery followed, and the hope that finally a Messiah must appear to restore their former independence grew stronger every day. Even the early Christians believed that the time was near when their Messiah would return. Sixty years had passed since; and as the first exile had lasted only seventy years, the conclusion was near at hand that again, after seventy years, a restoration would take place.

An excellent proof that the hope in the advent of a Messiah was rooted in political and not in religious ground, that the Jews did not expect a supernatural Messiah, but simply a man who would be their leader in the struggle for liberty, is that they prepared for the emergency. They were practical enough to observe that arms, ammunition, drilled men, and especially money, must be prepared and in readiness, so that the Messiah should have the sinews of war at his command. They did by no means believe that he was to work wonders, and do the fighting all by himself. They expected in him a leader, and nothing else.

The acknowledged head of the Jewish community at that time was Rabbi Akiba, whom I cannot help mentioning, as he played a principal part in the tragedy of the Bar Kochbean war. His history is wonderful, and reads like a novel. Up to his fortieth year, he is said to have been ignorant of letters, unable to read or write. His occupation was that of a porter in the house of Calba Sabua, the Vanderbilt of his time. At this advanced age, he fell in love with Rachel, his master's daughter. His affection was returned; but as Rachel well knew that her proud father would never consent to her marriage with a porter, and elopements were not fashionable at that time, she advised him, strange to say, to study law. Akiba heeded her advice, and began at the bottom of the ladder. He entered a primary school. During the many years of his studies, Rachel is said to have faithfully preserved her love for him, although her father, hearing of it, disowned her. She is said to have lived in such misery that once she was compelled to cut off and sell the braids of her hair in order to obtain money for food. Finally Akiba, who had risen step by step, gained renown; and, when he returned to Jerusalem accompanied by a host of disciples, and the acknowledged head of the Jewish community, Calba Sabua laid aside his prejudice, and gave him his daughter for a wife; bestowing upon her a rich dowry, so that from that time she could live in abundance.

Do you suppose that a man of the stamp of Rabbi Akiba, who not only believed in the divine origin of the Bible, but even maintained that every letter in it had a secret meaning: do you suppose for a moment that such a man did not understand the meaning of the prophets in regard to a Messiah, at least as well as Christian clergymen of to-day, who do not tire of quoting the Old Testament in support of their theories? If Akiba could have made one passage, yea, even one word, of Scripture tally with the appearance of Jesus as a Messiah, he would surely and willingly have accepted him. Or do you suppose that a man of such an iron will and as practical as Rabbi Akiba must have been, would have accepted the very first adventurer as a Messiah, that he would have sacrificed his influence, his time, his money, his life, for an impostor? This very Akiba, a second Samuel, pointed out Bar Kochba, and introduced him to the people as the long-expected Messiah. This very Akiba travelled for years, visiting all Jewish colonies, levying money and men for the Messiah. From one of his trips he is said to have returned with thirty thousand disciples, probably young men whom he had enlisted for his cause.

Bar Kochba, or Bar Kosiba, which name he derived from the small town of Kosiba or Kesib, was the embodiment of all the qualities expected to appertain to a Messiah. He was of powerful, herculean build; tall, muscular, strong. He was the model of a soldier. He would sleep on the bare ground, and share the coarse food of his soldiers. In battle he would be seen at the most dangerous points, whirling his battle-axe with undaunted courage. He was a skilful leader, who outgeneralled the most experienced soldiers of Rome. Deep as was his hatred for Rome was his love for his country. He was modest and willing to listen; and for all this his followers worshipped him. How he had passed his youth, where he had obtained his military knowledge, nobody knew. There he was at the time when all was prepared, and people were only waiting for the leader; and the impression which he must have made upon the people was such that, without examining his past record, all, the rich and the poor, the learned and the simple, flocked to his banner, and obeyed implicitly his commands. Within the space of one year he stormed fifty fortified places, and freed nine hundred and eighty-five towns held by the Romans; and when the year 133 dawned, not a single Roman was to be seen in Palestine.

At first the Emperor Hadrian, occupied with other schemes, gave little attention to the revolt; but when the most renowned legions had lost their prestige on Jewish battle-grounds; when his best generals returned defeated by a foe unknown before; when the Orient, observing that the Romans were not invincible, began to awaken from its slumber and to rally around the victorious Messiah, he tremblingly acknowleged the great danger that threatened the empire, and took immediate steps to suppress the rebellion at whatever cost. He ordered his best general, Julius Severus, the Moltke of his time, from England, where his presence had been needed, to proceed at once to Palestine. He gave him a large army of picked soldiers, and all the supplies he wanted. Bar Kochba, on his part, remained not idle during the two years which Severus needed to organize his forces for the task. He made an attempt to rebuild Jerusalem and the temple. He made use of the prerogatives of a king, and issued coins stamped with the inscription "Cheruth Jerusalem," Freedom of Jerusalem, a few of which are still to be seen. He fortified a number of cities, and was so confident of his final success that he is reported to have uttered the almost blasphemous words, "O God, if it does not please thee to assist us, withhold, at least, thy aid from our enemies; we shall then stand our own, and be victorious." Severus did not dare to meet his adversary in open battle. He adopted the same stratagem which Fabius the Cunctator had used against Hannibal. He refused to fight a battle; but he drew a large circle of fortified camps around the whole of Palestine, from which he sent his cavalry to tire the enemy in small encounters, and to cut off supplies. Bar Kochba had no horsemen to check the ravages of the Romans; and, in spite of all heroism, was not able to break the circle which Severus now contracted inch by inch. One Jewish fort after the other had to surrender for want of supplies; and soon the iron band closed around the fortress of Betar, into which Bar Kochba had been forced with the flower of his army. Betar must have been a city of the size of Metz; and the siege and defence of that city must have been a wonder of military skill. The two greatest generals of their time exhausted their genius in moves and counter-moves. Every inch of land was contested with bravery and skill, such as had seldom been witnessed before.

The Roman general finally despaired of capturing the city. Epidemics had decimated his legions; and though he had fought for a whole year before Betar, he had not gained the least advantage over his foe. He was about to raise the siege, when two Samaritan traitors showed him a secreted aqueduct which supplied the city with water. He shut the water off at once; but even the most excruciating pains of thirst could not make the noble garrison of Betar surrender the place. Not before the Romans had found a way into the city, by enlarging the same aqueduct, was the fate of Betar and that of Judea sealed. On a Sabbath day, Severus stormed the city. Bar Kochba, a second Leonidas, fell, sword in hand, covered with honorable wounds. He would not survive the final doom of his nation. A legend says that, when a man brought the head of Bar Kochba to Severus, and claimed that he had slain him, the latter said, "If this man has not been killed by God himself, the power of a mortal could never have harmed him." Another legend reports that his body, when found, was encircled by a snake, which would allow nobody to harm it.

Thus died Bar Kochba, a hero and a patriot. He would have sacrificed ten more lives upon the altar of his country, if such had been possible. Although he has been almost forgotten; although the masses have never heard of him; although our Christian friends are not aware of it, that the Jews once accepted a Messiah, and cheerfully spilled their blood in his service, because he was the type of that Messiah of which they had dreamed; although no poet has sung his praise, Bar Kochba is no myth. His history is written in the heart-blood of the nation upon the soil of Palestine. The Talmud contains numerous passages referring to him. Even the Gospels allude to him;* another indication of

* Mark xiii. 5-13. Take heed lest any man deceive you. For some shall come under my name, saying, I am the Messiah, and shall deceive many. And when ye shall hear of wars and rumors of war, be ye not troubled: for such things need be. For nations shall rise against nations, and kingdom against kingdom. . . . But take heed to yourselves, for they shall deliver you up to councils and in the synagogues ye shall be beaten. . . . Now the brother shall betray the brother, etc.

The *some* (τις) who was to assume the rôle of a Messiah, and of whom the faithful were to beware, is Bar Kochba, whose patriotism has not been without influence upon the Jew-Christians. The writer of Mark, who had witnessed the Bar Kochba revolt, puts the graphic picture of it into the mouth the time in which they were written. A Greek historian, Dion Cassius, speaks with reverence of him. There are still to be seen the coins which he had caused to be minted; and even the minutes kept by the Roman Senate bore evidence to his greatness. When Severus reported to the august body his final victory over the enemy, he omitted the customary introduction, "I and the army are well." Indeed, neither he nor his army was well. His victory had the semblance of a defeat. Neither did the Senate grant him the honor of a triumph.

Here we have a Messiah recognized by the people, recognized by its representative, Rabbi Akiba; a Messiah who laid down his life upon the altar of his country; but did Judaism make a God of him? Did it allow him to change one of its laws? Did he or his followers ever attempt to change a law, on the ground

of Jesus as a prophecy. The *wars* and *rumors of war* and the words *nations shall rise against nations* are not less descriptive of the Bar Kochba revolt and remind us of the occurrence of that time which Dion Cassius describes as follows: καὶ πάσην, ὡς εἰπεῖν, κινουμένης ἐπὶ τούτῳ τῆς οἰκουμένης. The passage, for they shall deliver you up to councils (συνέδρια), and in the synagogues ye shall be beaten, agrees with the statements of Justin and Eusebius, who say that Bar Kochba had punished the Jew-Christians because they would not fight against the Romans. Eusebius, in his history of the 17th year of Hadrian, says: Cochebas plurimos Christianos diversis suppliciis affecit, eo quo noluissent proficisci cum illo pugnatum contra Romanos. Compare Grätz, History of the Jews, vol. iv., note 15.

of his Messianic authority? Has ever a cult or a ceremony been instituted to commemorate his life and death? Though the Jewish nation has mourned him with bitter tears, his ill luck has made him share the fate of all unsuccessful! It is due to modern research that the marvellous career of Bar Kochba is brought to acknowledgment, and his heroic patriotism duly appreciated.

Although Rabbi Akiba had introduced Bar Kochba as the expected Messiah, he never attempted to make a tool of him. The confidence of the people rested in the qualities of the Messiah, and the recommendation of a man who had been the interpreter of the law for so many years only strengthened it. Rabbi Akiba survived the fall of Betar. It is said that he miraculously escaped before its capture, and that for some time he was the eye-witness of the sufferings through which his nation had to pass.

It has been claimed that the misery which had followed the Jewish nation was a punishment of God for their rejecting Jesus of Nazareth as a Messiah, and that it is a proof that they must have crucified him. How can such a claim be reconciled with the justice of God? How could our ancestors have acknowledged an unknown man, whose name was afterward used to change, if not to abolish, the law? Did they not show their firm belief when the man appeared who tallied with their expectations of a Messiah? Had they not all cause to believe in the Messiahship of Bar Kochba, better cause than they had to believe in that of the Nazarene? Had Bar Kochba not led the life of a conscientious Jew? Had he ever attempted to lead them from their inherited religion? Had he not been successful in the first years of the revolt? And as he showed all the qualities of a true Messiah, could they help believing in him? Was their devotion to him and his cause of no merit in the eyes of God? Was their heroism deserving of the cruel punishment which followed? Was it not rather deserving of reward? The argument that the Jews must have crucified Jesus because they have been persecuted since is simply absurd. Turn it around, and you will come nearer to the truth. Our history would have run quite smoothly if ignorance had not considered it an act of piety to make it fit with some alleged predictions; if our oppressors and persecutors had not considered it a high distinction to serve as the instruments of punishment.

But let me return to Rabbi Akiba. He was finally imprisoned on the charge that he had been an instigator of the revolt, and he suffered martyrdom from the hands of the Romans. The agonies of Jesus of Nazareth, if the narrative of the Gospels is admitted, are less than the sufferings of Rabbi Akiba, who was flayed alive. But in the hour of death, he did not despairingly exclaim, "My God, why hast thou forsaken me?" He died with the words on his lips, "Hear, O Israel: the Lord our God is *one* God."

Israel has never forgotten its noble heroes nor its martyrs. It has paid them their tribute of tears, and mourns them still: but it never made saints of them: it never worshipped them: it never preserved their relics and worked miracles with them; and this is the cause why the name of Bar Kochba has not become as familiar a household word as has the name of many another man of antiquity, who was far inferior to him in genius and patriotism.

The revolt of Bar Kochba was the last great military enterprise of our nation. After it, it ceased to be a political body; and its future history is that of a religious sect. We do not claim to-day to be a nation. The enlightened Israelite of to-day does not feel in the least chagrined that he has no country of his own or a king to rule over him. We are sincere and patriotic citizens of the country in which we live. We are good Germans in Germany, good Frenchmen in France, law-abiding Englishmen in England; and in this our glorious republic, which better than any other country in the world protects our liberties and our rights, we are true and faithful Americans, ready to prove it with our blood, if an emergency for such a proof should arise. We wish for no other country and for no other form of government; and all our efforts are directed toward the one great aim cherished by all true Americans, without distinction of race, color, or creed; the aim to make our beloved country respected and honored all over the world.

VI.

THE SPANISH INQUISITION.

A THOUSAND years are in the eyes of God as one day, sings the Psalmist; but in the eye of man, a millennium is quite a long time. If, therefore, I should pass over such a period in my research in silence, if I should take one great stride from the third to the thirteenth century without alluding to those centuries with at least a few words, I should be unjust to my task and at the same time lack a connecting link.

After the defeat of Bar Kochba, Israel, as I explained in my last lecture, ceased to be a nation, and became a religious sect. With this change, Messianic expectations lost their originally political character and assumed a philosophical form. Had it not been for the young Christian church, all Messianic Expectations would in all probability have then died out. The more, however, the church insisted upon the dogma that in Jesus the Messiah had appeared; the more it busied itself in digging out passages of the prophets which were to prove it; the more it interpreted and interpolated the Scripture to suit its purpose, the more our ancestors emphasized the doctrine that a Messiah was to come. Nor must we forget that the early church was actually for almost three hundred years expecting the return of their Messiah, and that thus in a natural way a similar notion was strengthened amongst the Jews. When finally Christ did not re-appear, the church changed its front. The Messiah being apparently unwilling to return to this world, his adherents went to him. Heaven with all its joys and a purgatory with all its infernal modes of torture were created. The Malchuth Shamajim, "the kingdom of heaven," originally denoting an era of universal happiness upon earth, was placed beyond the clouds, beyond the reach of the sceptic; and the wings of imagination, thus freed from the fear of the clipping shears of reason, grew and spread to an extent unknown before. Judaism knew originally neither of a heaven nor of a purgatory. Its laws were made to deal with "one world at a time"; and though immortality was not and is not denied by it, it shrank and still shrinks from the materialization or the description of a future life. Though it afterward became somewhat infected with these doctrines, its healthy condition did not allow the disease to spread; and intelligent Israelites have done away with such notions as they have with Messianic expectations.

The more Christianity embellished, frescoed, and decorated its heaven around the God-Messiah in the centre, the more clung Judaism to the belief in the advent of a secular Messiah, who should restore their nationality, take away the very opprobrium of their existence, and make them respected again in the world. But this was a mere doctrinal hope, if I am permitted to call it so. Like morphine, it soothed the pain, though it did not heal the wound. All kinds of chimerical ideas therefore gathered around it, as for instance, the resurrection of the dead, the stern judgment which the Messiah would hold over the world, and so on. It is a sweet consolation for the oppressed to hope against hope. Thus it afforded some consolation to our ancestors, when they were driven from country to country and were deprived of their human rights, to murmur: Wait till our Messiah comes; then we shall compare accounts.

During these thousand years, here and there and now and then an adventurer would appear, who would assume the rôle of a Messiah, gain some renown in small circles, and then disappear. In greater favor, however, were speculations as to the time when the Messiah was to come; and all kinds of reckoning were indulged in.

Some would count the letters of a Scriptural passage, others would endeavor to find that time by astrological calculations. Maimonides, who at his time was a rationalist of the first rank, the first philosopher after Aristotle who re-admitted reason into religious speculations: Maimonides, who at his time was as ferociously attacked by the Orthodox wing of Judaism as to-day he is enthusiastically quoted by the same party as its champion: Maimonides, to whom we owe the thirteen articles of creed, among which we find a plank inserted in favor of Messianic expectations, — this very Maimonides warns against giving such aspirations a practical turn. In a circular letter to the congregations of Yemen he proves to them that whenever these hopes had ceased to be hopes and attempts had been made to realize them, such attempts had always been followed by evil consequences.

As I do not intend to give the history of the Jews during this millennium, I shall with these few remarks dismiss that subject and turn to the topic which I have chosen for discussion, namely, "The Spanish Inquisition"; without which my next lecture, on Solomon Molcho, would be incomprehensible.

The Inquisition in general, and the Spanish Inquisition in particular, is, as all fair-minded people concede, an indelible stain on the history of the Christian church. No matter how many noble principles the church ever championed, the terror of the Inquisition forces them all into the background; no matter how radiant the halo is which encircles the brow of its saints, the names of Innocent III., Fernando Martinez, Torquemada, Ferdinand and Isabella, hang over it as a darkling cloud. The Inquisition has left its autograph upon the pages of history in such traces of blood that all the waters of the ocean cannot wash them away. For two hundred years and more hecatombs of human beings were sacrificed almost daily "ad majorem Dei gloriam," unto the greater glory of God. For two hundred years and more the smoke which arose from innumerable pyres upon which human beings were burned alive darkened the sky. For two hundred years and more human beings were systematically tortured and killed, for no other reason but that they differed in opinion with their oppressors. We can hardly understand to-day how humanity could have forgotten itself to such a degree; it is well nigh impossible for us to understand to-day how the church, which had proclaimed itself the champion of brotherly love, which had promised to extend love even to an enemy, could have so utterly failed in the execution of its principles, just when it stood at the zenith of its power. It is, therefore, worth while to look into the causes from which this phenomenal institution sprang.

It may appear quite a paradox to say that "Love" was the first cause for all the cruelties of the Inquisition. But let us be just and fair, no matter how much we have been the sufferers. Love was its first cause. During the twelve hundred years of its existence Christianity had developed in a manner which its innocent founders had never anticipated. Not to speak of the establishment of the trinitarian doctrine, of the changing of the Sabbath day from the seventh to the first day of the week, or of the introduction of saint and relic worship, the dogma of eternal happiness and eternal punishment, or, to call it by its right name, the dogma of heaven and hell, had been worked out in the most fantastic manner. The tortures and flames of purgatory were depicted in such terrifying colors that the stoutest heart trembled at the mere thought of them. The church maintained that man was conceived in sin; that therefore he was sentenced even before his birth to an everlasting abode in these infernal spheres; that the belief in the Saviour alone could snatch him from purgatory; and that the few drops of the baptismal water alone had the secret power to save him from the eternal fire. The rational thinker of to-day wonders that nobody at that time ever questioned how eternal punishment could be reconciled with the justice of God; but, it is a fact, nobody was ever struck by that idea, and for a long time even the absurd question was under earnest discussion, whether the souls of still-born children were to burn eternally or not. How firmly rooted these queer notions were, is to be seen from the fact that even Protestantism could not entirely part with them; that Luther threw his inkstand at the devil who appeared to him; and that even in this country witches were tried, sentenced, and burned. Even to-day only a small minority of our Christian friends, the Universalists and Unitarians alone, have practically denounced the dogma of eternal punishment.

These premises granted, it was indeed an act of "Love" to save a person from eternal damnation, even against his will, and by means no matter how disagreeable to him. The argument of the church basing itself upon this hypothesis was as sound as the hypothesis was absurd. The church would argue thus: The surgeon will inflict upon his patient momentary pain in order to save him from death; thus it is better to bring the momentary pain of the torture or the pyre upon a heretic than to allow him to pass into the eternal flames of purgatory, from which God himself could not then save him; or, as you will use the whip to drive cattle from a burning stable in spite of their struggles, thus the blind heretic, who does not see the flames which are awaiting him for all eternity, must be driven by force into the folds of the soul-saving church.

This motive of love may have actuated some of the inquisitors; and, in order to be fair, let us say many of them; for this motive is the only excuse for the horrifying cruelties committed. But so much is sure; it did not actuate all of them.

The second motive was "Fear." The church, which had built its structure upon imaginary props became timid when reason began to examine the foundation. So far it had dealt with barbarians, who were unaccustomed to reason. The Marionite monks had clubbed Greek philosophers to death; but they could not as easily kill reason. The spirit of scepticism with which an all-wise Creator has endowed man, the most beloved of all his creatures, began to move; and these motions were felt: they shook the foundation of the church. The Inquisition all over Christendom and also in Spain was not directed against Jews as such: it was directed against Christian heretics and against that element which, formerly Jewish, had turned Christian from compulsion and had now become the most troublesome and dangerous enemy from within. The church attempted to stamp out all rationalism. There was to be only one head and one will all over the world; namely, that of an infallible Pope, who could not err, and to whose decrees all humanity was to submit without giving them a single thought. But the spectre of Protestantism already haunted the chambers of the Vatican, and the Inquisition was resorted to in self-defence.

The Inquisition in Spain had still a third cause. In the beginning of the eighth century, the Mohammedans had entered Spain from the south and conquered it. The Christians had been driven to the northern part of the peninsula or to France, whence they kept up a constant warfare with the intruders. Though the Mohammedans had firmly established themselves on Spanish soil, and had civilized that country to a high degree, their days were numbered. Step by step the warlike Christians regained the lost ground. One castle after another, one city after another, was reconquered. The Jews, who had been tolerably treated by the Mohammedans, had arisen to a high degree of culture, and formed a large part of the population. They owned real estate and factories, carried on a large commerce, and rivalled even in chivalry their fellow-citizens, of both Christian and Mohammedan descent. While, however, the Moors could withdraw from before the pressure of the Christians to Africa or Asia, where their co-religionists were in power, the Jews had to remain; and their high intelligence, and still more their wealth, were looked at with envy by the poor and rude victors. They wanted their money, their houses, their fields, their factories.

The father of the Inquisition was Pope Innocent III., who ascended the papal see in 1198. He suggested a court before which all heretics, that is, all who differed from him, should be tried. But though at the same time he persecuted the Jews, who had become a living protest against the paganization of Christianity, the Inquisition as such had not yet occasion to deal with them. Its activity against Jews dates from a later period.

Ferdinand Martinez, a fanatic monk, was travelling through Spain on a missionary tour, preaching against all infidels in general, and against the Jews in particular. On the 15th of March, 1391, he preached in the market-place of Seville and inflamed the mob to a riot against the Jews, which, though stopped for the time by the government, was soon repeated. The Jewish quarters were stormed on the 6th of June in the same year; almost thirty thousand Jews were killed, and their dwellings sacked. Three thousand families saved their lives by submitting to baptism. The example of Seville infected all Spain; and riots occurred in every city, all with the same result. A part of the Jews were slaughtered; a few, after having escaped with their bare lives, eked out a miserable subsistence in obscure villages: the larger part turned Christians. Who could blame them if under such conditions they succumbed to the pressure of temptation? On the one side, death or the misery of the outcast for themselves and their children, on the other a life of respectability and affluence. All that was required of them was to suffer the rite of baptism, refrain from Jewish ceremonies and customs, and adopt those of the church in their stead. The Moors, who were not so scrupulous in regard to apostasy, gave an inviting example, and before long all Spain was full of Jewish and Moorish converts. A few more years and these converts had gained back by their intelligence, industry, temperance, and enterprise, what the mob had taken away from them. They soon formed the aristocracy, filled the highest offices in state and church; in a word, they soon became the rulers of the country.

It may be easy to accustom one's self to the thoughtless performance of some meaningless ceremony; but it is not as easy for one accustomed to reason to submit conscientiously to a creed inferior to his former one. A man may deceive others; but he can never belie himself. There was never a Jew at that time converted to Christianity who conscientiously believed in the doctrines of his adopted religion. They were all hypocrites, who had changed their creed for earthly considerations merely. They could not have been conscientious; for, although many may differ from me, I still maintain that Judaism is built upon reason, and not upon belief. The Jew is a born reasoner; he is a rationalist by his very nature; he is scepticism personified. The Spanish converts soon proved to be the most dangerous acquisition the church could ever have made. Although they went to mass and practised all the rites which their new religion prescribed, they did not believe in its doctrines: they ridiculed them as absurd; and infected with their sarcastic doubts their credulous friends. A riot once arose against them from an insignificant cause, which nevertheless illustrates vividly the condition of affairs at that time. There had been a drought in a Spanish district, and a famine was feared. A pious fraud produced some relic in which a light could be observed; and processions were formed to that shrine in order to ask the mediation of the saints for rain. While the credulous and superstitious populace bowed reverently before the miraculous relic, a pseudo-Christian sarcastically remarked that water would be better appreciated than the fire which the relic contained. He and his friends were mobbed.

The pseudo-Christians furthermore found a

certain charm in secretly observing the rites of Judaism. Secrecy always spreads a charm over the most insignificant matter. The boy who at his thirteenth year was secretly taken by his father to some obscure cave, and after giving several passwords was introduced to a congregation of pseudo-Christians and had to take a fearful oath that he would never betray them, must have been highly impressed with the unwonted ceremonies which he was invited to perform. The fringed cloak, the phylacteries which were given to him as a sacred trust, appeared to him the very essentials of Judaism, with which he now became much more infatuated than if all this secrecy had not been necessary. Associating with one another by means of their secret meetings, they naturally intermarried amongst themselves; and thus not even their race was obliterated. Their high intellectual abilities and the ambition which has always been a quality of the Jewish character installed them in the highest offices even of the church. There were bishops amongst them who would read mass in the morning, and, after having withdrawn to their closet, wrap themselves in their Tallis and most fervently read the Sh'ma. On account of their position and their wealth they were distrusted and hated by the population. They were called Marranos.

The mystery which surrounds this word has not yet been solved; but its general meaning was the accursed ones. With their former brethren the Marranos lived in some sort of friendship. They supplied them with teachers, and kept them in constant communion with Judaism.

The Inquisition found therefore in Spain a larger field than anywhere else. In other countries only now and then an incautious heretic would venture to raise his voice; but in Spain half the population were heretics. And heresy was to be stamped out at whatever cost. Whosoever was suspected of being a secret adherent of Judaism was brought before the inquisitory tribunal. The torture made the victim not only confess his own guilt but also the names of his co-religionists. Whosoever was convicted of heresy was robbed of his possessions, part of which went into the King's treasury, another into the coffers of the Inquisition, a third to the spy and traitor. If a victim of the Inquisition denied his guilt, he was tortured to death: if he confessed, he was delivered to the flames.

During the rule of Ferdinand and Isabella, the royal pair under whose government and for whose benefit America was discovered, an edict was issued which exiled every non-Christian, be he Jew or Mohammedan, from Spanish soil. Torquemada, the head of the Inquisition, is said to have wrung the consent to this edict from the timid king. An anecdote, for the truth of which I disclaim responsibility, but which appears not improbable, relates that while the edict was under discussion, Abrabanel, a wealthy and philanthropic Jew, had offered his whole enormous fortune to the king, whose greed for gold was well known, if he would refuse to issue the edict. The king seemed favorably impressed with the offer, and hesitated to sign the document. Torquemada at this critical moment, when the life and happiness of a hundred thousand human beings was trembling in the balance, forced his way into the king's cabinet. He held a crucifix in his hand, and addressed the king, in an angry tone, in the following words: "Jesus was sold once by Iscariot: now go and sell him again." The bigoted king could not withstand such a pressure; he yielded, and signed the edict.

The misery which followed defies description. Imagine a hundred thousand households broken up, their members deprived of all means of making a living, no country in the world ready to receive them, means of transportation scarce; while on the other hand it was not considered sinful, but rather an act of piety, to rob, murder, or sell into slavery the weary wanderers. Torquemada however, who thought to crush the Marranos with this blow, also was mistaken. Thousands of Spanish Jews perished at that time; thousands of others succeeded in reaching other countries; but the majority remained. They embraced Christianity, and swelled the ranks of the Marranos. How they must have loved their new religion can easily be imagined. The Jews having been removed, the Spanish Inquisition had now to deal with the Marranos only. The task was not an easy one, and the battle was fought with skill and fanaticism on both sides. Nor were the Marranos permitted to convert their property into money and leave the country. The very suspicion that one intended to depart was sufficient to indict him, rob him of his property, and sentence him to grace the next auto-da-fé with his presence. The papal court grew rich from bribes which both the Inquisition and the representatives of the Marranos offered to prevent edicts in their favor or disfavor.

This persecution was continued during more than two hundred years, until the last of the Marranos had either died in the dungeons of the Inquisition, or expired on the pyre, or made good his escape. And what was gained by this persecution? Reason was not suppressed; the very Marranos were the secret promoters of the religious revolution which was soon to take place. After many a defeat, Protestantism gained the victory. It had come to stay. But Spain, rich in itself, and still enriched by the rain of gold which America showered upon it, grew poorer every day. Her population grew up in ignorance and bigotry, and never learned how to use money properly. Her best, her most intelligent and enterprising citizens, had been driven away; and she degenerated to her present condition. The Jews and the Marranos exiled from Spain aided the rise of England and the Netherlands. In the same degree that Spanish cities declined, the cities of Holland and England grew in wealth and prosperity. The policy of the Inquisition had been a suicidal one.

The miseries through which our ancestors had to pass during these two centuries in that country made them naturally look for aid from without; and Messianic expectations became again the order of the day. Any adventurer who would have assumed the rôle of a Messiah would have found a willing ear, support, and followers, at that time.

Two men, on occasions working together, at other times acting independently of each other, produced the greatest sensation at that period, and caused quite a stir among both Jews and Gentiles. It has not yet been decided whether David Rubeni and Solomon Molcho were adventurers, impostors, or deluded partisans; but their history is so marvellous, so romantic, so fascinating, and at the same time so unknown to the public, that I shall, in my next lecture, give a short sketch of it.

VII.

DAVID RUBENI AND SOLOMON MOLCHO.

DISCOVERIES and inventions are of such frequent occurrence in our days that nothing less than the discovery of a road connecting the earth with the moon would startle us; and even then we should easily overcome the surprise and naïvely ask, "What next?" Whenever we are informed by the press of a new invention or discovery, no matter how far-reaching in its consequences, we take such news as a matter of course: as something that we had a right to expect of the inventor or discoverer.

Such indifference may appear abnormal and discouraging; but it keeps us cool and level-headed. If the reported discovery or invention does not rest upon a solid foundation of probability, we dismiss it at once as a fabrication, and give it no further attention. Imagination has become subordinate to reason in our days.

A few hundred years ago such indifference did not prevail, and every new discovery addressed itself rather to human imagination than to human reason. The discovery of America by Christopher Columbus set the world almost wild with astonishment and surprise. Not alone that a new continent was added to the world, not alone that all the former theories as to the shape of the earth were at once annihilated: the newly discovered country, with its strange plants, strange animals, and still stranger human population, showered at once such a rain of wealth upon Spain, the happy land which had been instrumental in its discovery, that the imagination of all Europeans became heated to the highest possible degree, and the most fabulous narratives of travellers found eager listeners and enthusiastic believers. Nothing seemed impossible after such a discovery. The city fathers of Genoa and the princes of Portugal now blamed themselves for not having listened to the plans of Columbus; and they, as well as the rest of the European princes, were ready to invest in the most adventurous schemes, simply because they were afraid of losing another chance, and because the most incredible stories now seemed probable.

The interior of Africa, though much better known to-day than ever before, is still shrouded in mystery; and the exploits of the late Mahdi, the siege and capture of Khartoum, the failure of England to liberate the heroic Gordon, and what is of still greater weight, the uncertainty as to the final fate of the general, are proofs that we have still to learn a great deal about these far-off regions. Five hundred years ago these countries were still less known to the Europeans.

In the year 1524 a man arrived at Venice via Palestine and Egypt, who claimed to have come from the interior of Africa. He gave his name as David Rubeni; he said that he was the brother of Joseph, a Jewish prince who ruled over a large kingdom, the inhabitants of which were no others than the descendants of the tribes Reuben, Gad, and Manasse. Joseph, as well as he himself, according to his genealogy, was descended in a direct line from King David. He was in possession of credentials of the Jewish government and of letters of recommendation of Portuguese residents: he also carried a silk flag upon which the ten commandments were embroidered, and he spoke no other language than a corrupt Hebrew, which the European Jews could hardly understand. He said that he was charged with a message to Pope Clement VII., who had ascended the papal chair in 1523. Although he himself did not say much about his errand, his attendant gave the secret away, that King Joseph, David's brother, had an army of three hundred thousand well-drilled soldiers in readiness to fall upon the Turks and to reconquer Palestine; but that he was in need of fire-arms and ammunition; and that therefore he had sent his brother to ask them of the Pope or of any other prince who should be willing to invest in the enterprise. He furthermore reported that gold and diamonds were in his country of no value whatever, as the precious metal and the costly gems were so common there that people would not pick them up, and children only played with them. David pretended never to have studied any Jewish book, but claimed to be a soldier by profession. He bragged that he had killed with his own hand forty men in one single encounter. The good people of Venice listened eagerly to these reports, and never doubted a word. David was a homely looking fellow, of small stature and swarthy complexion. He was no orator whatsoever, but must have possessed a peculiar quality of brazen-faced presumption. At Venice he shrewdly avoided his co-religionists and remained in the house of the sea-captain who had brought him from Alexandria. His attendant, however, drew attention upon him; people called at his residence and considered it a great honor to be admitted into his presence and to aid his enterprise with money. A rich Venetian Hebrew, Mazliach or Felix by name, received from him the honorable distinction of acting for him in the capacity of a banker; that is, to discount the notes which he drew on his brother

Joseph. After a short rest, David proceeded to Rome. Riding a snow-white horse, and accompanied by his attendant and an interpreter, he appeared at the gates of the Vatican, and to the surprise of all was immediately admitted to an audience before the Cardinal Giulio. A few days later the Pope himself received him, and accepted his credentials. These papers were sent to the court of Portugal for examination, and were promptly returned from there as genuine documents. The Pope thereupon treated David with the honors and courtesies due to an ambassador, and consulted him almost daily in private conferences.

Pope Clement VII. was one of the best popes who ever graced the papal throne; but he was also one of the most unfortunate. He lived at a time when all Europe was in a state of chaotic disorder. The Reformation, which had begun with Luther, had spread all over Europe and had found a stronghold in Germany. The German Emperor, Charles V., being at the same time King of Spain and ruler over the newly discovered America — a prince in whose realms, as the saying was, the sun would never set — wished to humble Italy and to press it down to a secondary position in the council of nations. This made the position of the Pope difficult. If he should oppose the Emperor's secular policy, Charles was likely to encourage Protestantism in retaliation for the papal resistance; if, on the other hand, Clement should win over the Emperor to his plans in regard to the suppression of heresy, he would be obliged to make concessions at the expense of the Italian prestige. Nothing short of a crusade against the Turks could help the Pope out of his dilemma. At a time when the most impossible seemed to be possible, when anything was believed, David's story was not at all discredited by the Pope; for there was an opportunity for him which he could not afford to lose. An army of three hundred thousand soldiers ready to be sent against the Turks was the very thing he needed.

Palestine granted to the Jews, there remained the rest of the vast territory of the Mohammedans to be divided, for which purpose a crusade could easily be preached. The Pope, placing himself at the head of the undertaking, would regain the lost prestige of the Roman church, Protestantism would be forgotten amidst the din of arms, and the ambition of the Emperor would naturally be turned away from Italy into other channels. All these advantages could be obtained for a few guns, a few barrels of gunpowder, and a little toleration shown to the Jews.

If the Pope, the head of Christendom, thus treated a Jew, what could be expected of the Jews but that they should become frantic with joy? The greater the misery which they had lately suffered in Spain, and which the Marranos were still suffering there and in Portugal, the more did they cling to the hope of restoration held out to them, as it appears, by a shrewd adventurer. This again shows that the Messianic expectations of our ancestors were of a political and not of a religious nature. The idea that the Messiah was to remove the sins of the world is a Christian invention; and the most believing of the Jews never believed in that doctrine. Their Mashiach was expected to be a king, who should restore their political independence, and nothing else. Just at the time when their misery seemed unbearable, when their existence was threatened with total extinction, they received the welcome news that there existed a Jewish king, a descendant of David; that this king commanded a large army; that he was immensely rich; that he was ready to assert his influence in their behalf; and that he was about to reconquer Jerusalem and to re-establish a Jewish kingdom. No matter whether the report was true or not, whether they were the dupes of an adventurer or not, such were exactly the hopes which they held in regard to a Messiah. And, after all, as long as the Pope believed in the man and treated him with courtesy never shown a Jew before, why should they not believe in him?

Under the given conditions they were justified in expecting some grain of truth in his statement, even if the bulk of his stories should be fictitious. They crowded around Rubeni, and supplied him with all the money he wanted. David played his part in a masterly manner: he kept the crowd at a respectful distance from his person, showed no signs of greed for money, and made such an impression upon the giver that he considered himself happy when his donation was accepted by David.

No practical results, however, were reached by all the secret sessions which he held with the Pope; and the latter allowed him to depart, when a letter of invitation arrived from the court of Portugal for him.

Joao III., of Portugal, a king who ruined his country by his greed and stupidity, who knew of no higher policy than to fill his purse, no matter at whose expense, wished to introduce the Inquisition into his domain, for no other reason but that it was a well-paying institution. Portugal was then as full of Marranos as was the neighboring Spain; and Joao looked with envy across the boundary lines at the harvest which the Inquisition yielded there. The Pope, however, notwithstanding his urgent demands, was not ready to give the necessary permit. While the Portuguese court and the Vatican were in communication, and both the court and the Marranos tried their utmost to get the Pope on their side, Joao had heard of the appearance of Rubeni and of his errand. He changed his policy at once, and invited him to Lisbon, with the view of making a treaty with him. Rubeni, who apparently must have been very liberal in his promises, received from the king the assurance of his aid. Five vessels loaded with guns and ammunition were to be given to him in consideration of an amount of money and commercial advantages specified in a secret clause. During the time in which this important business was transacted, David was treated by the king like a prince; and all the edicts against the Marranos were cancelled.

This unfortunate class of people, living in constant danger of losing life and property, tormented by the pangs of conscience, surrounded by bigotry, fanaticism, and superstition, had finally lost all self-control. A great many of them had become mentally so deranged that they would believe in the most absurd notions. When Rubeni appeared at the court and was received with such high distinction, thousands of Spanish Marranos escaped to Portugal; and they all hailed him as the Messiah who would save them from their unnatural position, and restore both the Jewish nation and religion. All eyes were directed longingly at him, in the expectation of the wonderful events which were to happen.

A young man of noble family of the class of the Marranos, a youth of rare beauty, of poetical genius, and of a commanding power of speech, became so highly impressed with the appearance of Rubeni, and the hopes connected with him, that he made himself unknowingly a tool in the hands of the adventurer. Diego Pirez, born in the year 1501, was about twenty-four years of age when Rubeni arrived in Portugal. Born among the Marranos, he had received an excellent education. He spoke several languages fluently, and was not ignorant in Hebrew literature. He held the office of a clerk at the royal court of justice, and stood in great favor with the government. Nothing else was known of him before; but no sooner did Rubeni appear than Diego Pirez had all kinds of dreams and visions in regard to the advent of a Messiah and the future of the Marranos. He approached the adventurer in order to find out directly of him whether his plans would correspond with his visions. Rubeni, as usual, remained cold, and did not betray his plans. Pirez thought he should win his confidence by his open return to Judaism; an act which was punishable with death. He performed the Abrahamitic rite on himself; and the loss of blood which followed caused a dangerous fever, during which Pirez had again frightful visions, all relating to the appearance of a Messiah who was to save the Marranos. He even thought he heard the voice of an angel, who appointed him for that mission. From that time he changed his name, and called himself Solomon Molcho, which is about the same as King Solomon. Having thrown aside the mask of Christianity, he could no longer remain at home. He escaped and fled to Palestine. The young enthusiastic Marrano who had had the courage to return openly to Judaism created quite a stir in the Orient. He gave himself out at first as an ambassador of David Rubeni, but later as the Messiah himself; and his dreams in which he foresaw his early death, and that he should be sacrificed as a burnt offering to God, were the constant themes of his lectures, which were listened to by thousands of people, and afterwards (in 1529) printed in Salonica. The substance of his addresses was always the same, namely, that at the end of the year 5300 of the world, or 1540 of the new era, the Messiah would appear; that Rome would be destroyed, and Jerusalem rebuilt. His fame spread, and all kinds of fantastic hopes were connected with his name.

In the meantime, King Joao III. again changed his policy. Without giving any cause, he notified Rubeni to quit Portugal within two months, and began to urge the papal court to establish an inquisitory tribunal in his kingdom against the Marranos. Clement hesitated. He could not arrive at conclusions, partly because he abhorred the crimes committed by the Inquisition, and partly because the suspense was valuable to him, as both parties appearing before him did not come with empty hands.

About this time, Solomon Molcho arrived in Ancona with the intention of going to Rome to convert the Pope to Judaism, even at the risk of his life. In Rome he secluded himself for thirty days, fasting and praying, and again had visions. He foresaw that a great flood would submerge Rome, and that Lisbon would be destroyed by an earthquake. Of these visions he spoke in the synagogues of Rome every Sabbath; and it seems that the Pope himself began to believe in him. The fact remains that Clement VII. not only received him frequently in audience, but protected him against his enemies. The flood which he had predicted and the earthquake of Lisbon occurred in fact; and the Pope no longer doubted his divine mission. It is said that once the Pope saved Molcho's life, when the Inquisition had taken hold of him and had sentenced him to be burnt in public, by substituting another criminal for him, and secretly aiding him in his escape.

In 1531, we find Molcho in Venice again in company with Rubeni, who dealt with the city council as he had formerly dealt with the Pope and King Joao III. All of a sudden both men conceived the adventurous idea of travelling to Regensburg, where the Emperor had called a diet, in order to convert him to Judaism. Charles granted them a few audiences, but soon imprisoned them and took them to Mantua, where both were tried on charges of heresy brought against them. Diego Pirez was sentenced to death upon the pyre. At the last moment a messenger sent by the Emperor offered him his life if he would repent and return to the church. Molcho answered that he was pleased to offer his life to God as a martyr; that he repented one act only; namely, to have believed in his own Messiahship. He died without a murmur. Rubeni, who could not be sentenced as a heretic, was taken to Spain, and died in the dungeons of the Inquisition, after the torture had made him confess the names of a number of Marranos,[1] who were burned in consequence. The hopes, however, which had been linked to his name and that of Solomon Molcho did not die out for some time. Not before the year 1540 had passed away without a Messiah making his appearance were these hopes relinquished.

Although only a comparatively short time has

elapsed since: although the art of printing must have facilitated the establishment of facts: although the printed sermons of Solomon Molcho and a diary of Rubeni are still extant, the queer career and still queerer actions of these two adventurers are still clouded in mystery. Their connections with the Pope, with the King of Portugal, with the patricians of Venice, with the Emperor of Germany, are historical facts; and still nothing definite is known about their transactions with these influential persons. Their history, fabulous and romantic as it may appear, contains, however, a few points which bear unmistakable evidence to the correctness of the propositions which my lectures on Messianic expectations are to advocate.

First,—The Jewish conception of a Messiah, as long as such hopes were indulged in, has always been the same; namely, that of a man who would restore the national existence. The theories of hereditary sin, of eternal damnation, of redemption through the Messiah, have always been rejected as absurd by the Jews, even at the time of the Inquisition, when the wildest confusion of ideas was prevalent on account of the Marranos, who had inhaled the doctrines of both Christianity and Judaism.

Second,—Messianic expectations, at the time of Rubeni and Molcho, show already the traces of old age. They had already lost their strength and their fervor. Hopes were indulged in, but no practical steps were taken to realize them. These hopes, even, would have vanished had they not been kept alive by the persecution from which our ancestors were suffering at the time. If Messianic expectations had not been on the decline, they would have borne better fruit at that peculiar historical period than the fantastic exploits of Rubeni and Molcho. The whole excitement did not last longer than about eight years, and was confined to Spain and Italy only; and, after all, it affected the Christians more than the Jews. A pope, a king, and the aristocracy of a renowned city seem to have been the dupes of two Jewish adventurers, while the Jews only lost a small sum of money.

Third, — It appears to me that the Messianic character which was attributed to both men was an invention of their friends, a blind to cover the true inwardness of their mission. It seems to me that they were nothing but the secret agents of the Marranos to work at the courts of Rome, Lisbon, and Regensburg in their favor; and that when both had lost their lives in their dangerous mission, legend took hold of them, and surrounded them with a wreath of marvellous deeds. It seems that they worked conscientiously for their cause, and not for private gain. There is no trace to be found that they lived extravagantly, or that they amassed money. They drew their necessary expenses, which were little; and the rest of the money intrusted to them was consumed in bribing the corrupt courtiers whose influence was needed and could not be obtained otherwise.

These points evidently prove that Messianic expectations must have been the temporary hope of a merely political character, which had practically died out with the occasion which had produced them; namely, with the loss of the Jewish nationality. They furthermore prove that these expectations never took the form of a doctrine, and never supported the structure of Judaism. They were fanciful decorations on the outside of the building, but were never essential to our religion.

Another cause which perpetuated their life for some time was the Kabbalah, a disease which was caused by the unhealthy atmosphere in which Judaism was compelled to live, a cancer which had slowly but steadily spread over its whole body, and almost caused its death. At the very time when all Europe shook off the torpor of the Middle Ages, and began to inhale the morning breeze of the new day, Judaism was stretched on the sick-bed with that disease; and if we have not yet gained a more respected position in the communities in which we live, it is due to the delay in our advancement caused by that sickness.

As the Kabbalah has also produced a would-be Messiah, the last one of repute, I shall introduce his history by a lecture on the Kabbalah, its origin, growth, and evil consequences.

VIII.

THE KABBALAH.

THERE has never been an individual or a nation which has been altogether original in its thoughts or actions. We call the productions of an author original in so far as the same subject has never been treated before with the same strength and in the same words; but if you enter upon a close scrutiny, you will find that the greater part of them is the reflex of ideas current at the time of the writer, and that even the few for which originality is claimed are the product of a combination of inherited sentiment, study, and special accidental impressions. The secret of the success of an able writer and speaker is not to be found in his originality, but in just the opposite; in that he gives expression to the ideas of his readers or hearers.

We constantly give and take. No matter how secluded a person lives, his thoughts will be influenced by his surroundings: no matter how deeply a nation is sunk in barbarism, it cannot withstand the influence of civilization brought upon it by other nations with which it happens to come in contact.

There is perhaps no nation on earth which has come in contact with a greater number of others, and has stood in a closer relation to them, than the Jewish nation. It has mingled with Egyptians and Phœnicians, with Assyrians, Babylonians, and Persians, with the Greeks and the Romans, and with all the modern nations. Its record dates from the time when the Pyramids were built, and can be traced through all ages to this very day. It is therefore no wonder at all that its originality was affected by its surroundings, that it has worked into its system the popular notions of all the peoples which I have enumerated, and that it was influenced by the current ideas and philosophies of the different ages. It is an undeniable fact that though we have given, we have also received; that though we have influenced others, we have been influenced by them in turn. It is a grave mistake on the part of our friends to think that Judaism has remained intact and unchanged from the time of its origin until now, and that the Israelites of to-day hold the same views as did their great-grandparents two thousand years ago. A great many ideas, good ones as well as bad ones, have found their way into Judaism, which were by no means essential to its spirit. After they had been absorbed, they hardened within its system, and the historian of our days, who examines the phenomenon, wonders now how such a strange matter could have ever grown so deeply and firmly into the living wood that it is almost impossible to remove it without harming the tree itself.

The religion of the Babylonians and that of the Persians exerted their influence upon Judaism, as well as the Egyptian cults, which stood godfather at its cradle. By degrees the theories held by the Parsees of God and the world crept into Judaism; and the loom of time worked them into the Jewish tissue. From the time of the intercourse with these nations we find that a belief in the existence of supernatural beings, in angels of light and darkness, springs up in our religion; that it develops, and that by the side of the commandment, "Thou shalt not make any representation of any being, be it in heaven or on earth," the most fanciful descriptions of the heavenly regions are indulged in. At the very time when the Babylonian Talmud was near its completion, a mystical book appeared, the Sefer Jezirah, the book of Creation, in which not only the different classes of angels are named and their daily duties minutely recorded, but in which the writer does not shrink from describing the throne of God, and from capping the climax by giving a measurement of his limbs. The length of his beard, for instance, is given at ten thousand five hundred Persian miles. Such notions were surely not Jewish, but still they were held by our ancestors. There is not one philosophical system known which has not left some traces in the structure of Judaism; and while at times the rational system of Aristotle predominated, there were times when mysticism ruled supreme.

Maimonides, the exponent of the twelfth century, the greatest philosopher of his time, had returned to the Aristotelian system, and attempted to interpret the Bible in a rational manner. He was the outspoken enemy of mysticism; he denied the existence of miracles, and endeavored to explain the Mosaic laws and rites from a scientific point of view. This rationalism created a storm of indignation in orthodox circles, which broke forth with still greater violence after his death. It raged for two hundred years, and became finally the cause of a reaction, of a return to mysticism, and of the origin of the Kabbalah.

The burning question of those days was exactly the same one which is debated to-day, namely, the divine origin of the Bible. Starting from the belief that God himself was its author, the question arose how its discrepancies could be accounted for. How could a divine author admit into his book passages like that of Lot and his daughters, that of Judah and Thamar, and others? What was the use of a legislation which in course of time had become impracticable? There remained only two courses: either to say that the Bible was the work of human authorship, or to find a key by which it could be read in a different way. Maimonides would have chosen the first way, had he lived longer. The second way seemed to most the best; and, as necessity is the mother of invention, the key was produced. A secret meaning was attributed to every word of the Bible, which could be obtained by changing the letters and substituting such others for them as would represent the same numerical value. It must be understood that every Hebrew letter represents a number. The first ten letters of the alphabet stand for the numbers from one to ten; the next ten stand for the tenths; and so on. Each word has, therefore, a numerical value. Supposing, now, that the letters of a word would give the number 120; the Kabbalist could substitute any other word for it, provided its letters would also count up 120. This system opened the door to an unbounded mysticism. The rationalism of Maimonides was silenced at once: the Bible now became, in the hands of a clever Kabbalist, the proof of everything, no matter how absurd; and an entirely new religious system began building upon this hypothesis.

The world, imperfect as it is, was said not to have been created by God, the Perfect, the Infinite, who was called in the language of the Kabbalah the "En Sof;" but that between this world and the Supreme Being there were ten circles, or "Sefiroth," of which God, the En Sof, formed the centre. The substance of the first circle which had emanated from God was similar to him, but not exactly like him: the second was the effusion of the first, similar, but not like it: the third of the second, and so on, each Sefirah growing farther from perfection. The visible world was the effusion of the last circle; and by means of these circles, which were flowing into one another like the colors of a rainbow, man stood in connection with God, and God with man. The En Sof was infinite; but the Sefiroth were finite. The En Sof had no bodily form; but the Sefiroth had a spiritual and bodily form, and through their medium God could appear in a visible form, and reveal himself to man.

The human soul was a citizen of this higher world, and stood in direct connection with the Sefiroth. It could, therefore, exert an influence upon them, and through them upon the highest divinity. A noble soul could force the En Sof to send his blessings through the channels of the Sefiroth upon this world; while a wicked soul could hinder the divine activity. Good actions would facilitate, ignoble actions interrupt, the divine effusions. Every rite and every ceremony was of mystical importance: they were the instruments to influence the divinity. The prescribed daily prayers were positively effective provided they were directed to the proper Sefirah. All prayers were to be addressed to them, and not directly to the En Sof. The formula of the prayer was alone of importance, not its meaning and sense. By means of the prayer the Kabbalist could work miracles.

All souls were said to have been created from the beginning as the residents of the Sefiroth. Every soul was preordained to a union with a body, and for a life in this world. In this earthly career it was to prove that in spite of its union with a body, it could preserve its celestial purity. If a soul was successful in this life, it ascended forever into the higher spheres; but if it succumbed to earthly temptations, it had to return again and again to this world until finally it had passed its earthly life in perfect purity. Most of the souls, however, were forgetful of their heavenly origin; and thus it happened that most of the souls on earth were old ones who had lived there before. New ones were rarely sent to the world, because, as the number of souls on earth was limited, no new soul could be started until an old one had returned forever to a higher sphere. The Kabbalist could tell at sight whether a person was a new soul or an old one. Not until all souls had passed their earthly existence, and had returned to their heavenly abode, would the end of days be reached, when all souls and all the Sefiroth would again be absorbed and drawn in by the En Sof. The soul of the Messiah would be the last one to appear; and his advent could, therefore, be accelerated or retarded by the goodness or depravity of mankind. In all these fanciful doctrines we can easily discern, not only the traces of Persian mysticism, of Buddhism, and of Mohammedanism, but also the prevailing Christian theories; as, for instance, the power of prayer when directed to a mediator who stood between God and man, and the possibility of an incarnation by means of the Sefiroth. All these doctrines were secretly transmitted from teacher to pupil. A Rabbi Isaac, called "the blind," Rabbi Asriel, and Rabbi Jehuda ben Jakar, and Nachmanides, the most inveterate antagonist of Maimonides, are named as the first teachers of the new science.

This science, however, could not at first gain a firm foothold; for it lacked authority. People would ask, How do the Kabbalists know all these things? How do they know that their key is the right one? But this deficiency also was soon to be supplied.

Rabbi Mose ben Shem Tob de Leon, born at Lyons in 1250, was a man of inventive genius. He eked out a miserable life by copying books. He was a spendthrift, and always pinched for money, at the same time unscrupulous as to the means of getting it. He had learned a little of everything, but had never acquired thoroughness in any study. He had studied the Kabbalah too; that is, the few doctrines which then were taught. When he found that an appetite for this study was springing up amongst his contemporaries, he wrote several treatises on that subject. He failed, however, to win glory or money from the literary productions which appeared under his own name. The idea once struck him that a Kabbalistic book which should appear under the name of a recognized authority might have a ready sale. As author for such a book, he selected Simon ben Jochai, a rabbi of great renown, who had lived in Palestine in the second century, and of whose ascetic life a number of legends had survived. He was said to have lived for nineteen years as a hermit in a cave, to have fasted six days in a week out of the seven, and to have received direct revelations from God. The teachings of this rabbi, if written in the Chaldean language, the language of the Talmud, would not be doubted. Mose de

Leon went to work, and one day he surprised his friends with a copy from a manuscript which, as he said, had been discovered by Nachmanides in the grave of Simon ben Jochai. He had sent it to his son, but a storm had carried it to Spain, and from there into his (Mose's) possession.

The book was entitled the "Sohar," which means splendor, and was divided into several chapters, having no connection with one another. It was filled with the most fantastic and absurd narratives. Angels and devils, Paradise and Gehenna, played a prominent part therein. The souls were traced through all their wanderings; and their mystic relations to the Sefiroth and the En Sof were considerably dwelt upon. All this knowledge of the spiritual world had been obtained by revelation. Simon ben Jochai, the alleged author of the book, had learned these secrets from God himself. God himself had instructed him how to use the key to the Bible, and how to read it correctly. By means of his ascetic life, he had penetrated Sefirah after Sefirah, until he had been in direct communication with the En Sof.

The Messiah was not ignored; he was to appear in the beginning of the fourteenth century, and by this statement the clever counterfeiter betrayed himself. He ceased to be the anointed king who was to restore the political *status quo ante;* and he became in the Sohar a mystical being, the incarnation of the En Sof, the exact image of the Messiah taught by Christianity. And still such theories were called Jewish. The demand for the book increased; but Mose de Leon did not reap the fruits of his labor. He died. The original manuscript was now demanded by the influential men of that time, but could not be found. Mose's widow insisted upon it that her husband had written the whole book himself. The Sohar became, nevertheless, an authority. Its origin from Simon ben Jochai was never questioned. Soon the new revelation overgrew Talmud and Bible, and the night of mysticism lulled the Jews into a magnetic slumber.

We may well ask how it was possible that the common sense for which the Israelites have ever been noted could have become so thoroughly suppressed as to let them accept such an aberration of the mind; a book which bears the traces of fraud right on its face.

Well, it is the most impossible which is generally sure to happen. Our imagination is quicker reached than our reason. Mysticism always has had a secret charm over mankind; and even to-day, in our enlightened age, there are thousands who, in spite of all exposures, believe in Spiritualism, in clairvoyance, and other mystic absurdities. At that time there were added some other reasons, of still greater force. First of all, the proud spirit of our ancestors had been broken by constant persecution. A man whose life and property are constantly endangered loses naturally the force of reason, and grows superstitious. Soldiers, sailors, and highway robbers, are as a rule the most superstitious people on earth. The law which compelled our ancestors to wear a peculiarly shaped hat, or a yellow spot on their outside garment, and thus had made them a constant target for ridicule, had destroyed their self-respect, and had made them low-spirited and dull. Furthermore, their neighbors were as superstitious as they were. The spirit of mysticism at that time held the whole world under its sway. The Crusades had opened the eyes of the western barbarians to a civilization in the east of which they had never had a conception. Whatever they saw of adroit mechanism in Constantinople or eastern cities they took for the secret work of evil spirits. For instance, they could not understand why some people looked up to the stars and made charts of the night sky. They believed that astronomers received information from the stars in regard to the future of man. Astronomy was changed into astrology, in which even men like Wallenstein believed. Geometry, not known before in western Europe, puzzled the uncultured barbarian; and he thought a secret power was attached to the triangles, squares, and circles, of the mathematician. The medical art, which was not known in western countries, but had its seat in the east, remained a conundrum to the Crusaders. Every botanist and every physician seemed to them to be in secret communication with superhuman forces. The belief spread that it was possible to change base metals into gold; and the cradle of our chemistry was alchemy. All these absurdities were, however, the fertilizers which stimulated the barren ground, and brought forth all our modern sciences; but the scientist of that age had to work and to experiment in secrecy. The church felt instinctively the danger which would arise for it from these studies, and stigmatized science as the black art, as the machination of evil spirits. It persecuted and ostracized as sorcerers and enchanters all those who would indulge in such studies, and compelled them thus to carry on their researches in secret, in the darkness of the night, which aroused still more the superstition of the populace.

It is, therefore, not at all surprising that the same symptoms made themselves visible on the Jewish body, as it suffered from the same sickness; the difference was that these absurdities were worked out in a peculiar Jewish manner by our ancestors. Numerous commentaries on the Sohar were produced; all the secret arts, as necromancy, astrology, and alchemy, were drawn into the Kabbalah; and an abundance of impostors arose, who claimed to be in possession of King Solomon's ring, and to possess power over the spiritual world. These impositions would have done little harm had not the study of the Kabbalah overtowered finally the study of Talmud and Bible, destroyed reason, changed the whole religious system, created and introduced new ceremonies, which were palmed off as truly Jewish; so that finally Judaism could no longer be identified in the form in which it then appeared.

Our present orthodoxy is the last remnant of the Kabbalistic age. What our orthodox brethren defend as Judaism is Kabbalism. Many of the prescribed prayers, the number of which was not to be abrogated, are of Kabbalistic origin: most of the ceremonies still in use among them were produced in the age of the Kabbalah. The New Year's day and the day of Atonement, formerly days of joy, received a gloomy character, which still prevails. The Kaddish prayer, which reform has not yet been strong enough to abolish, but which it has at least modernized and rationalized, is a relic of that age, and was supposed to hold a mystic power over the souls of the departed members of the family. The words of the Kaddish prayer, which in their simple form contain a glorification of God, were supposed to contain an entirely different meaning when read with the key of which the Kabbalist was the owner. The burial rites, with all their superstitious practices, still in use among our orthodox brethren, are an offshoot from the Kabbalah. Even I remember the time when Kabbalistic amulets were still in use and were placed over the cradle of a new-born child to prevent evil spirits from harming it. And all these superstitious rites were and are still called Judaism!

The Kabbalah clung by necessity to Messianic expectations; but the most fantastic and absurd hopes were connected with his appearance; and if there are still Jews living who conscientiously believe in the coming of a Messiah, they believe in the Kabbalistic Messiah, and not in the Messiah originally expected at the time of their political depression.

It is now about one hundred years since the reform movement began (with Moses Mendelssohn); and its blows were directed first of all against the Kabbalah. From the time that Israel was relieved of that incubus, it began to live again and to reconquer its lost position in the world. All the present difficulties which we experience in the strained relations between orthodoxy and reform are due to the rapidity of our progress during the last hundred years.

We had overslept ourselves, and had to make up for lost time. Our present reform does not intend to harm Judaism, for it loves it; but it is compelled to blast the last remnants of Kabbalism, which by the ignorant masses are taken for Judaism.

The Kabbalah has produced a Messiah such as could be expected of it; a man who did more harm to Judaism than any previous Messiah. He was as great an impostor as the Kabbalah was an imposture; and still, men like Baruch Spinoza, the greatest philosopher of his age, did not know what to make of him.

Sabbatai Zwi, the last Jewish Messiah on record, filled for the last time the hearts of his contemporaries with the delusive hopes of national restoration, and afterwards alienated thousands of his followers from their religion. His activity falls in the middle of the seventeenth century; and, although his history gives evidence that he was a mixture of fraud, mysticism, and self-delusion, it is as romantic as that of any of his predecessors, and gives a true picture of the Kabbalistic swindle by which his time was imposed upon.

IX.

SABBATAI ZWI.

THE struggle between darkness and light, as witnessed at the dawn of every day, is a sight well worth seeing. It seems as if two giants were wrestling with each other for the supremacy over the world. While the eastern horizon assumes a pale roseate hue, deep darkness still hovers above the western sky; and it appears as if armies of clouds were despatched from there toward the east to suppress the rising light. Then a mixture of light and darkness spreads for some time over the world, in which all objects take on the most fanciful appearance. Finally, the clouds recoil from before the arrows which the rising sun sends from his radiant chariot against them, objects become discernible in their true form, and the world hails the victorious day.

The seventeenth century is in more than one respect comparable to that struggle between darkness and light as experienced in nature at the dawn of every day. The night of the Middle Ages begins to withdraw from before the light of the new era, but not without a struggle. That peculiar mixture of light and darkness which we call twilight was then hovering over the intellectual world. In its dim light, all facts appeared distorted, though their true forms could already be distinguished. The press, the influence of which was then already felt, was yet in its infancy. It was fed with nourishment that had grown stale by the time it reached it. A statement, fallacious or untrue, because it could not be rectified at once, grew more harmful when spread by the press than it would ever have been before. Journalism, that branch of the press which to-day is called *the* press, had scarcely seen the light of the world: it existed in an embryonic form, lacking both hands and feet — telegraphs and railroads. While the names of Descartes and Spinoza, of Kepler, Galileo, and Copernicus appeared as the messengers of the new day on the one side of the horizon, the deep night of mysticism was still beclouding the world; and both Jews and Gentiles were still held in a deep slumber by its magnetic influence.

In one of my previous lectures, I have already stated that Christianity in its earlier days had been expecting the return of Jesus; and that this notion had been the cause of similar Messianic expectations among the Jews. These hopes, long forgotten among Christians, were all at once called into life again in the beginning of the seventeenth century. The Thirty Years' War, then raging in Germany, the rise of Protestantism, the inroads which the Turks were making upon Siebenbürgen, the discoveries which were so surprising to the unintelligent; all these causes combined revived these old, long-forgotten hopes. The Christians, both Catholic and Protestant, all at once believed that the world would come to an end, and that Christ would re-appear at that auspicious moment. From some obsolete prophecies it was figured out that the fearful catastrophe was to occur in the year 1666.

The Jews were soon infected with the same mania; and the Kabbalists now discovered that the passage in the Sohar which had predicted the appearance of the Messiah in the beginning of the thirteenth century had been misinterpreted, and that the proper time for his appearance was about the same as that of their Christian neighbors, namely, the year 1648. Then their Messiah would come, riding upon a lion, reconquer Palestine in a miraculous manner and without arms, and establish the Kingdom of Heaven. By that time, the Kabbalists said, the last lot of souls would have arrived on this sublunary world, and with it the soul of the Messiah; and everything would then be in readiness for the absorption by the En Sof.

From that time dates the pernicious custom, which is still prevalent among the Jews of Poland and Russia, of marrying off their children at the early ages of from ten to fourteen years. It was introduced in order to exhaust the quicker the supply of unborn souls, and thus to accelerate the arrival of the Messiah. In Smyrna eight hundred such juvenile couples were once married on one day. When Rabbi Manasse stood before Oliver Cromwell and pleaded the cause of his brethren, asking permission for them to immigrate into England and to settle upon her soil, one of his arguments was that, after all, their sojourn would be of a short duration, as the time was near at hand when their Messiah would appear. This shows that even practical men of the stamp of Rabbi Manasse were infected with the craze and dared to speak of it as a matter of course to the Protector of England, who in turn received this reference to the current and popular belief in the same spirit in which it was given.

During the war between the Turks and the city of Venice, the commercial relations of that city had become so unsafe that large English and Dutch firms removed from there and established branch offices in Smyrna. Mordachai Zwi, a Jew of Spanish descent, who had removed to the same place from the southern part of Greece, opened a commission business there representing the interest of several English houses. His strict honesty and his clever management won for him the confidence of the firms for which he acted, and made him a rich man. On the 9th of the month Ab, the memorial day of the destruction of Jerusalem, in the year 1626, a boy was born to him, whom he called Sabbatai. The child grew up to be a handsome young man, who, both by his comeliness and by his intellectual qualities, gained the sympathies of all. He was a remarkable boy. He would withdraw into solitudes where he could give full swing to his imagination. He never mingled with his fellows, nor would he ever join in their games. For a short time he studied Bible and Talmud; but soon he left these studies and was initiated into the mysteries of the Kabbalah. The ascetic life which was demanded of a Kabbalist suited him extremely. He would pray and fast and meditate and bathe at nights with such a promptness and minuteness that before he had reached his twentieth year he had already become the master of a small circle of disciples. He had, however, one peculiarity which distinguished him from other Kabbalists and surrounded him at the same time with a still brighter halo of holiness. He was totally indifferent to the other sex. Although he had married, according to Kabbalistic usage, at an early age, and his wife was very pretty, he never lived with her as man and wife; so that she asked for a divorce, to which he raised no objection. With the same coldness he afterwards treated his second wife. His father worshipped him, and ascribed his success in business to the influence which his son was able to exert upon the En Sof. This made Sabbatai conceited; and as a Messiah was expected about that time by all, it occurred to him that he and no other was that distinguished personage. On his twenty-second birthday, in the year 1648, he made himself known to a select circle of friends and disciples as the long-expected Messiah, by pronouncing the four-lettered name of God as it is written. The Kabbalah had predicted that the Messiah alone would dare to pronounce this name in the same manner as it was pronounced before by the high priest. When the rabbies of Smyrna heard of it, they grew indignant; and their college, the Beth-Din, excommunicated him and his followers. The fact was that they loved to dream and to talk about Kabbalistic nonsense, to hope and to pray for a Messiah, but were not ready to face the creations of their own imagination when they appeared before them in broad daylight. After a quarrel which lasted for several years, he and his disciples were exiled from Smyrna.

The prompt action of the rabbinical college

ought to have nipped all his Messianic aspirations in the bud; but it had just the opposite effect: it stiffened his backbone. The conception of a suffering Messiah, borne and tenderly nourished by Christianity, had crept by that time into Jewish thought: he considered his persecution to be an essential part of his Messianic mission; and being well supplied with funds by his father, he scorned the interdict of the rabbinical synod of Smyrna; and his illusions grew with every new day.

It is not exactly known where he stopped and what he did during the next fifteen years. A few traits only have survived. On his travels he once met a wandering preacher who at the same time was a copyist of note. His name was Abraham Jachini. From him he received a piece of old parchment, upon which the following inscription could be seen, in old-fashioned Hebrew characters: "I, Abraham, was imprisoned in a cave for forty years, when I heard a voice saying, In the year 5386 of the world (that is, 1626) a son shall be born whose name shall be Sabbatai. He shall humble the dragon: he is the true Messiah: and he shall wage war without arms."

It is not known whether this piece of penmanship had been made to order, or whether Jachini, who had heard of Sabbatai's assumption, had written it for the sake of mystifying the mystifier. Sabbatai accepted the document as genuine, preserved it, and proved by it his mission. In the year 1653 we find him in Salonica surrounded by a host of admirers. Here he prepared a peculiar farce. He celebrated his wedding with a scroll of the law such as you can see in any Jewish synagogue. On this occasion he proclaimed himself as the Messiah, — and, mark me well, as the son of the En Sof, — who by order of his father was to marry the law, the daughter of heaven. This scene, carried out with theatrical pomp, so enraged the sober part of the Jewish population of Salonica that he was driven ignominiously from that place.

He then travelled through Greece; but the congregations, which had heard of his excommunication and his vagaries, would not allow him to stay with them. Strange as it may appear, all these difficulties tended to increase his presumption and to raise his courage. From there he went to Egypt. In the capital, Cairo, there lived at that time a wealthy Israelite. He held the highest office in the land; for he had leased the revenues and taxes of all Egypt. Raphael Joseph Chelibi was as charitable as he was rich, and as credulous and superstitious in matters of religion as he was shrewd in business affairs. Fifty Kabbalists were supported by him year in and year out; and whosoever was in want appealed to him. He was the Rothschild of his time. While he was transacting an immense business, he fasted and prayed and chastised himself with a lash made of wire, all for the sake of hastening the advent of the Messiah by his ascetic life. Sabbatai initiated him into his secrets, and made a faithful friend of him. In 1663 he went to Jerusalem; as it seems without any reason, and for no purpose whatsoever. As the year 1666 was approaching, he probably believed that his presence might be needed in the Holy City at that eventful time, and that perhaps some miracle would occur in his behalf upon the sacred soil of Palestine. But though he observed the most rigorous asceticism, though he bathed in the Jordan river, and visited the graves of the patriarchs, no miracle occurred. His circle of admirers even did not widen to any extent; when all of a sudden an accident happened which made him famous at once. An oppressive tax had been imposed by the Pasha upon the Jews of Palestine, which they were unable to pay. They were threatened with extermination if the money should not be paid at the appointed time. Sabbatai offered his services as a messenger to the charitable Raphael Joseph in Cairo. His embassy, as could be expected, was crowned with success; for the charitable gentleman subscribed the amount which was needed; which, however, was attributed to the influence of Sabbatai, the Messiah, upon Raphael. But he obtained even another opportunity to prove his Messiahship.

In far-off Poland a whole Jewish colony had been butchered years before by the Cossacks. One little girl only had been saved, by accident. She had been found the next day by a benevolent person half starved and almost frozen to death, who gave her up to the sisters of a neighboring nunnery. Here she grew up to be a maiden of rare beauty; and though she had been instructed in the tenets of the Christian religion, she still remained, so she said, a Jewess at heart. One night this girl was found by some Israelites almost naked on their burial place. She claimed that the spirit of her father had taken her in the stillness of the night and carried her through the air from the cloister to this place. He had told her that she was to become the bride of the Messiah. To the astonished Jewish women she even showed the finger-marks which her father's spirit had left on her body. The Jews, being afraid to get into trouble for her sake, did not investigate the matter, but sent her to Amsterdam, where, she said, she had a brother. She remained for a few years in Amsterdam; then went to Frankfort-on-the-Main, and later to

Livorno, always claiming that she was to be the bride of the Messiah. She did not, however, lead such a life as would be becoming to such a distinguished person; for in all these cities she bore an ill name. Whenever the inconsistency of her behaviour was shown to her, she would say that because she was to become the wife of the Messiah her irregularities had been allowed to her by divine revelation. The story of her adventures had reached Cairo; and Sabbatai at once corroborated her story, claiming that he had been waiting for her appearance as she had for his. He sent for her, and in the house of the generous Raphael their nuptials were consummated in gorgeous style. This marriage made him at once a Messiah, and he justified his queer action by referring to the prophet Hosea, who likewise had been ordered by God to marry a lewd woman. His fame spread, and his glory was still increased by an addition of a few satellites who were pleased to shine by his side. A Kabbalist called Nathan Ghazati assumed the rôle of the prophet Elijah, who was to be the forerunner of the Messiah, and two other Kabbalists, Sabbatai Raphael and Mathatias Bloch, travelled for him, preached in his name, and proclaimed him as the true Messiah. About this time Sabbatai began to bring system into his enterprise. He kept a regular court, in which Sarah figured as queen. He withdrew himself from the gaze of the populace, and appeared only on high festive occasions in public. He employed a private secretary, who sent official documents in the name of the Messiah to all Jewish congregations in Europe, Asia, and Africa. He now returned to his native city, entered it triumphantly; and on the New Year's day, 1665, he proclaimed himself publicly in the synagogue of Smyrna by the sound of the Shofar as the long-expected Messiah. The enthusiasm soon developed into a craze. Men, women, and children began to prophesy: miracles occurred every day and all over the country, and the mania spread like wildfire. In Holland, England, Germany, and Poland, wherever a Jew lived, whom the glad tidings of the appearance of the Messiah reached, the wildest hopes arose: business was neglected; estates sold out; and delegates loaded with money were despatched to the court of the Messiah. The greater the number of these legations grew, the greater appeared the dignity of the Messiah; and as every delegate could truthfully report the conflux of people, and the magnificence of the court, and as these reports of unbiassed eye-witnesses could not be doubted, the mania spread wider and wider, and the Messianic fever grew more intense. A banker in Amsterdam who had uttered some irreverent remarks about the Messiah suddenly fell down dead, and the belief of the credulous crowd in the miraculous and far-reaching power of the Messiah could never be shaken after this accident. In England bets were made for and against him, and the betting stood one hundred to ten in his favor. Heinrich Oldenburg, a German scholar of great renown, did not know what to make of it, and predicted a great change in all public affairs. Even Spinoza, the Pantheist, acknowledged the possibility that the Divinity might again have chosen Israel as the bearer of the moral law. Christians began to doubt their own religion. If Sabbatai was the true Messiah, as he then appeared to be, what was Jesus of Nazareth? Many Christians turned Jews in order to be on the safe side in 1666.

There was only one man at that time who remained sober in the general delusion. Rabbi Jacob Sasportas of Hamburg raised his voice of warning, which, however, was drowned in the frantic turmoil of that peculiar time.

If Sabbatai had been a man of some sense, if he had possessed some character and some power of will, he could have made something out of the feverish enthusiasm which then had taken hold of everybody; but he was no man of ability or of genius, he was a self-conceited impostor. He did nothing; he lived *in dulce jubilo* from day to day, waiting for a miracle. He divided the world among his followers. To one of his friends he gave Poland, to another Germany, and Raphael Joseph Chelibi received Egypt for his share. So firm was the belief of his deluded followers in him that they would not sell their shares for enormous sums of money, which, in fact, were offered to them. He pretended to know the souls which inhabited their bodies. One of his friends was the soul of King Solomon, another that of King Joas. He furthermore changed the Jewish holidays; he made the ninth of Ab, his birthday, a day of rejoicing, and did away with the day of Atonement. He gave himself out finally as the incarnation of the En Sof; that is, in plain words, he said he was God himself.

The swindle had now lasted long enough in Smyrna; and the Sultan, or rather his vizier, Achmed Kopriti, thought it high time to see to it. Sabbatai was summoned to appear before the Sultan, in Constantinople. At the beginning of the year 1666, he set sail for that city. After a stormy voyage, he landed near the Golden Horn, and was immediately imprisoned by the Turkish authorities. When questioned about his Messianic pretensions, the coward denied them, and said he was merely a Jewish rabbi who had been delegated to collect alms for Jerusalem. Kopriti, who at that time was in need of Jewish money for the wars which he was waging with several European powers, and who had the good sense of not making a martyr of a man who was a harmless impostor, gave him the small castle of Abydos as his place of residence, where he was to be kept as a prisoner of state, under guard of a Turkish officer. The castle now became a second Mecca. From all parts of Europe pilgrims arrived; and a rain of gold was showered over the whole neighborhood. The leniency with which the Sultan treated him was interpreted by the admirers of Sabbatai to mean that he was powerless to harm the Messiah, who had dared to approach him unarmed and unaided by an army. The belief spread that the Sultan would soon abdicate in Sabbatai's favor; and it almost seems as if Sabbatai himself had believed in his supernatural power. His impudence, however, led to his early downfall. Ambassadors had come from the interior of Poland to ascertain the truth of the Messianic rumor. They told him that in their own country a man had predicted the coming of a Messiah, but had named another person. Sabbatai haughtily ordered these delegates to send that man to him. Nehemia Cohen, the Polish prophet, obeyed the order, and appeared before him. After a long conversation which he held with the Messiah, he denounced him as an impostor. Sabbatai's followers, to avenge the insult, attempted to murder Nehemia, who, however, escaped from their hands, went to Constantinople, turned Mohammedan, betrayed to the Sultan the secrets of the Messiah, and gave him advice how to put down the excitement at once without making a martyr of the swindler. Then he escaped from Constantinople, returned to Poland, became again a conscientious Jew, and vanished from the public as suddenly as he had appeared.

The Sultan, acting on the advice of Nehemia, demanded of Sabbatai a token of his Messiahship. He would shoot three bullets at him at close range. If he should remain unhurt, he would acknowledge him as the Messiah; if not, he should be killed at once, if the bullets had not yet finished him.

Sabbatai, as could be expected, most respectfully declined the honor of being used as a target for the royal rifle-practice, and instead turned Mohammedan. He took the name of Mehmed Effendi, and received a good salaried office at the court of the Sultan in exchange. The Jews throughout the Ottoman Empire were punished with a heavy taxation; and Sabbatai was used as a tool to convert them to the religion of Mohammed. When, after some years, he was found out to be rather lax in his devotion to his new religion, he was banished to a far-off village, where he died unnoticed and in obscurity, in the year 1676.

But the mania of which he had been the exponent and the cause did not die as soon. His admirers could not believe, and would not believe, that the Messiah had betrayed them. They announced the dangerous doctrine that it was allowable to change the form of religion; and thousands of Jews, who had lost their property during the mania, and were now ridiculed into the bargain, after the bubble had burst, turned Christians or Mohammedans. Others were still expecting the return of Sabbatai; they still clung to the Kabbalistic nonsense, which, however, had now lost forever its former strength.

After this Messianic failure, Messianic hopes fell to the freezing-point. They were upheld theoretically, they found expression in prayers, they were uttered mechanically with the lips; but they were discarded practically, and found no longer an echo in the hearts of our ancestors.

This era of mysticism was the last struggle between darkness and light. The sun of reason rose higher and higher, and all these spectres vanished from before it. Kabbalism, too, had to go. Mendelssohn and his contemporaries destroyed it with their logic. Even Christianity changed its front. The American and French Revolutions gave freedom to the Jews, and offered them full citizenship, which so long had been denied to them; and with this offer, not only their homesickness, — their yearning after a land of their own, — vanished, but also all Messianic hopes passed quietly away.

At the very same moment when the old bellman's grandson shouted up to the belfry, "Ring, ring, grandpa! Oh, ring for liberty!" and when the old state-house bell of Philadelphia spread with its metal tongue the news that the United States had declared their independence, the Messianic idea heaved its last sigh. At that auspicious moment its soul passed away, and what was left of it was a lifeless corpse, which has for some time lain in state, but which now is buried for good.

X.

CONCLUSION.

THE human mind is the manifestation of God in man. It is as infinite as is the source from which it sprang. Though chained to a body of clay, it rises above space and extends beyond time. Time and space, the limitations of the body, cannot imprison the mind. Carried by the wings of imagination, we can roam not only through all the periods of past history but also through all the ages which are still to come. In an instant we can travel thousands of miles; and without experiencing any unpleasant sensation we can change our residence from the frigid north pole to the torrid equator.

The moments when our mind, escaping from the prison-cell of the body, roams through the infinitudes of time and space are the happiest in its earthly existence: they are marred only by the thought that it must soon return into the cage, and exhaust itself again in its daily work, in the treadmill of reality.

Conclusion.

In a series of these mental excursions we have followed the trail which an idea, the Messianic idea, has left upon earth from the time of its inception to that of its demise.

Let us now draw the conclusions, now that all the evidence has been brought in.

We have found, first of all, that the Messianic expectations of the Israelites assumed shape not merely once, but several times, and in different historical periods; a fact which is not known to the public in general. Four or five men, from out a large company, have gained renown as Messiahs: Jesus of Nazareth, Bar Kochba, Rubeni, Molcho, and Sabbatai Zwi. Their careers varied in particulars, but there is an astonishing resemblance to be found in the main features of their lives. The early history of all of them is shrouded in darkness. Like the gods in Greek mythology, they step forth suddenly out of the mist of a cloud. They appear, and nobody knows whence they come. After a life of short duration they all disappear in a similar manner. With the exception of the last one, none of them died a natural death. Jesus died despairingly on the cross; Bar Kochba heroically on the battlefield; Molcho was roasted alive; Rubeni died in a dungeon; and Sabbatai Zwi died ignominiously in exile. None of them reached an advanced age. Sabbatai, the oldest of them, died at the age of forty-one years; Solomon Molcho, the youngest, at thirty-one. Jesus is said to have died at the age of thirty-three years. Bar Kochba's age cannot be ascertained; but he must have died a young man. None of them, with the exception of Sabbatai, was married, and none of them left children.

Neither was any one of them a creative genius. They never dominated their time: on the contrary, they were carried away with the current. They never moved the masses; they rode on the crest of the popular wave. They were merely the supply to a public demand. Their Messianic assumptions, sincere or hypocritical, became possible only on account of a popular hope in the appearance of such a person. None of them appeared at a time of national prosperity; they all without exception stepped upon the stage in times of calamity. They could grow only upon ground fertilized by misery. Whenever the national wretchedness had become unbearable, whenever the spirit of the people had become so depressed that they despaired of themselves, the hope sprang up that help must come from outside, from above: that a man must appear who would improve their condition. But at such times of calamity the human judgment becomes biassed, and the reasoning powers lose their normal strength. A drowning man will cling to a straw: so a nation in despair will cling to the most childish hopes.

None of the Messiahs ever improved the state of affairs: on the contrary, they all left the nation in a still greater misery than they had found it. This, too, is a cause why so very little is known of any of them. Had they lived in times of prosperity, when their actions could have been judged in calmness; had they been able to improve the condition of their friends, morally or materially, we should have heard much more of them. The facts would have been sifted; and we should have received them in an authentic form. But the hardship of their times was so great that nobody thought of fixing dates or of establishing a historical fame for them; and after the clouds had passed away it was too late to collect the material and to clear the truth from fiction.

The Messianic idea is the child of Judaism thus far only, that during the time when our ancestors formed a small nation and their political existence was threatened with extinction by mighty oppressors, they hoped that a man would appear among them who would liberate them from the yoke of the foreigner and restore their national independence. After the defeat of Bar Kochba, when the last glimmer of that hope was extinguished, the child naturally died; but Christianity the daughter, be it to console her mourning mother or be it for a more selfish reason, exchanged the dead body for that of another child, to which she herself had given birth. This grandchild, sickly as it was, was by mistake nourished by its grandmother thereafter until now this child died too. All Messianic expectations which were indulged in by the Jews after Bar Kochba were un-Jewish, and were excusable only on the plea of homesickness, from which our ancestors suffered for seventeen hundred years, owing to the inexcusable treatment which they received from the hands of their prejudiced neighbors.

I can understand Messianic vagaries of a political character, I can understand that a nation oppressed by a mighty foe, and unable to break the yoke by its own efforts, experiences a certain consolation in the hope that some one will come and liberate it; but after a people has lost its national existence, after its children have been scattered all over the earth, and have lived as citizens of other countries, for almost two thousand years, it is absurd even to think of a national restoration. I fail to see the benefit which the Jews would derive from the re-establishment of a Jewish commonwealth. The mere attempt to realize such fantastic hopes would be followed by evil consequences. Palestine, to the possession of which we are said to be entitled, is not as large as Massachusetts:

it could hold two or three millions of inhabitants. What, now, would become of the seven millions of Jews which could not find room therein? Furthermore, in what respect would our condition be improved? Could a Messiah uphold our civil rights better than President Cleveland did in his first message? Behold the dependent position of the small Danubian countries; behold how these princes are mere puppets in the hands of their stronger neighbors, and how the resources of these countries are squandered in wars which will never benefit them; behold these conditions, which would be our own, and then compare them with our standing as free citizens of this free republic. Do we not share the legislative power with our fellow-citizens? Do we not hold the ballot in our hands? Do not Israelites hold offices in the municipal and national government? Are not life, liberty, and the pursuit of happiness granted to us as well as to any other citizens of this country?

It is told of Julius Cæsar that he once displayed his ambition by saying he had rather be the first magistrate in a small village of Gaul than the second in rank in Rome. I say, and every intelligent American Israelite will support me, that we would rather be plain citizens of the United States of America than the leading statesmen of a Jewish commonwealth in Palestine.

Two important points, however, yet remain to be answered. One is generally brought forward by our Christian friends; the other by our co-religionists.

Our Christian friends claim that we are mistaken in tracing the Messianic expectations of the Jewish nation to a political basis. Although they concede that at the time of Jesus the Israelites may have expected a politician or a soldier as their liberator, they uphold the theory that such a Messiah was not needed: that the mission of a Messiah is not a local one, but that it is universal. The Jews, they say, in their eagerness for national redemption, overlooked the fact that the messenger of God had come to redeem the whole world.

Now, in order to show that we are not hasty in our conclusions, that we feel keenly the gravity of this question, and that we are willing to handle it with all possible care and tenderness, let us suppose for a moment that the Christian sources are authentic: let us suppose that our Christian friends of to-day do know better what our ancestors needed eighteen hundred years ago than they did themselves: let us suppose that the gospels were written by Jewish eye-witnesses, and were never tampered with by copyists; and that the life, the words, and the deeds, of Jesus are correctly represented therein. Let us furthermore suppose that it was his mission to redeem the whole world not politically, but from its sins and iniquities.

Starting from this supposition, are we not justified in expecting of such a divine messenger that first of all he would reveal to the world new laws, better than the former ones, new doctrines, superior to those to which the people adhered before? Now, were the utterances of Jesus new? A very large part of what he is reported to have said had been said before him: and he repeated it. Many and many of his teachings can be traced to previous Jewish sources. What he taught was Judaism plain and unalloyed. Not one paragraph in his sermon on the mount contains anything that could have been new to his hearers. He was not even a reformer; for he is reported to have said distinctly that he was not come to change or to abolish the Mosaic law. Not one attempt was made by him to establish a new religion or to lay down a plan for the redemption of the world. Although he does not conceal the traces of mysticism which his connection with the Essenes had left upon him, he lived and died a conscientious Jew; and none of his followers derived from him the least right to deviate from the example which he had given to them. It is a fact conceded by our Christian friends that he did not realize the hopes of his contemporaries, not even those of his disciples; that he did not improve the condition of his nation, either by his life or by his death. But did he save the world? Did he remove sin? Has humanity become perfect through him?

Think of the barbarism of the Middle Ages; think of the paganization of Christianity; think of the atrocities which have been perpetrated in his name; the cruelties which have been committed for his glorification; the wars which have been waged for the propagation of the religion named after him. Observe human passions still impeding the path of virtue: read the list of crimes committed every day; and then say that the world has been redeemed of all evils: speak it out unblushingly, if you can, that sin has been removed and that humanity has become perfect since the time of his death. The best proof that the alleged Messiahship of Jesus was a failure on earth is that its result, the predicted redemption of the world, has been removed to heaven, to spheres of which we have no knowledge whatsoever. Whatever our fate may be after death, be it immortality or annihilation, it is in vain to go into any controversy about it, as none of the disputants know the least thing about it. I wish, however, with all my heart, that the hopes of our Christian friends in regard to the soul-saving qualities of their faith may be realized in what they call heaven, as completely they have so far been a failure on earth.

If mankind has advanced in knowledge, if the standard of morality has been raised, such has not been the work of Jesus, nor that of Christianity alone. Thousands of good and noble men and women, and all religions on earth, from superstitious fetishism to radical agnosticism, have worked together for that end. If we have progressed, if humanity is better to-day than it ever was before, if a better sense of justice prevails, if the cruelties of war have been mitigated, if crimes have been suppressed to some extent, we must not fail to consider the enormous influence of the host of inventors who have discovered the secrets of nature, and have made its powers the obedient servants of man. The inventors of steam-power, of electricity, of gaslight, of machinery, of the printing-press, — they have been among the real saviors of humanity; for they have removed, though indirectly, more sins than the combined efforts of all religions have been able to weed out. They have stormed and broken down the barriers of caste and creed; they have wrenched the sceptre from the hands of despots, both secular and spiritual, and have caused the establishment of the right of every individual to participate in the government of his own affairs.

They have alleviated the wrongs of life, so that the poor of to-day is a wealthy man compared with the poor of the past. Their rails and electric wires have tied humanity into one large community, and through their agency all human beings have learned to regard one another as brethren, and to share the joys and woes of their fellow-beings from pole to pole.

It is a fallacy to regard the past as the time when people were better, nobler, happier, than they are to-day; it is a mistake to seek for ideals only in the past, after which to shape our conduct in the present. Not disregarding filial devotion which is due to a parent, I claim that we are better and happier than were our ancestors, and that future generations will be still better and happier than we are. The ideal of the present man ought to be the man of the future, not the man of the past.

Thus the Messianic idea of universal redemption, brought forward by Christianity, collapses. Jesus has not been the savior of his nation; and, as far as the last eighteen hundred years have proven, he has not saved the world. Our ancestors,— provided they had known of him, — could not accept him as a national Messiah, because he did not tally with their expectations; and we cannot now or ever accept him as a universal Messiah, as the savior of the world, because he is not the ideal which we have to-day of such a person.

The other point raised by our co-religionists, who, as it seems, only for the sake of opposition, will not concede that the Messianic idea is dead and has been finally buried with Sir Moses Montefiore, is of apparently still greater importance than that which I have discussed just now.

The preservation of Israel, they say, would be a waste of providential care : the sacrifices which our ancestors have made upon the altar of their religion, the miseries which they have patiently endured, the blood which they have spilled, would all be in vain, if our cause should not finally triumph ; if in the end we should not only regain a political independence, but even become the aristocracy of the world. The whole drama would close abruptly without the grand finale in which our patience and endurance should be rewarded.

There appears to be some logic in this point ; but appearances frequently deceive. First of all, it is absurd to speak of a waste of providential care. There is no waste in nature nor in the whole government of the universe. The term "waste" is applicable only to human affairs. The purpose for which a being is preserved is not always that which we in our human blindness expect. We may call it as well a waste of providential care if an oak tree that had been growing for a thousand years, and had withstood the storms of ages, is consumed by a forest fire instead of being sawed into beams and boards, and used for building purposes.

The sacrifices which our ancestors have made, and the miseries which they have endured, were made and endured by them for their own sake, and not for the sake of the future. They could not submit to the views which another religion wished to press upon them; and, therefore, they rather suffered than yield. We would do the same to-day; and there is no religious sect which has not done the same. It is a poor argument to say that we must be Jews, and suffer humiliations of all kinds, merely because our parents have been Jews, or because our great-grandchildren will sometime receive the reward for our patience and endurance. We cling to Judaism because that religion suits us best; because it answers all our purposes. We transmit this religion to our children not for the sake of aiding God in the accomplishment of some purpose, but because we think they will be as happy in this religion as we have been, are, and shall ever be; that they will become noble members of the human society by adhering to its principles. If a man is not sincerely a Jew, if he does not firmly hold that Judaism rests upon a solid foundation, he commits a wrong if he hypocritically instils into his children principles which he does not subscribe to himself; and if he should think that another creed than the one he has inherited is better and more likely to make him or his children better and nobler, he ought to embrace it, the sooner the better.

There is an inconsistency in these Messianic hopes. On the one hand, it is expected of the Messiah to introduce a government of peace and equality, a time when all shall do the good for the sake of doing good; when all passions shall be silenced, when love shall unite all humanity in one great brotherhood, and when the same God shall rule over a happy world. On the other hand, however, it is hoped that there would be some distinction after all; namely, that we should be raised to the highest plane, that our opinions should prevail, that our God should be *the* God. If the rest should not be inclined to acknowledge our superiority, then, of course, we should regret it exceedingly if we were compelled to make them submissive by some sort of punishment. It may be a pleasing play of our imagination to dream of a time when we could speak to our fellow-citizens somewhat in the following strain: You have never believed that we were right; you have never been ready to grant us the position to which we were entitled. Now, the tables are turned; now, we are the masters : but we shall not pay you in the same coin ; we shall be satisfied with the mere acknowledgment of our superiority over you. Such dreams may gratify our vanity ; but they are idle. Those who expect to indulge in such selfish vanities will be greatly disappointed. If it should ever come to pass that the religious thoughts of mankind became uniform, you may rest assured that at such a time none of the present religious systems would be prevalent. The religion of the future will be neither specifically Jewish nor Christian nor Mohammedan. It will be an entirely new system, in which the immortal parts of all the present religions will be represented, but at the same time so equally balanced that none will dare to claim superiority. A Messianic period with one of the present religious systems dominating is an absurdity, and a contradiction of itself.

We may, however, boast, if boast we must, that, as Christianity and Mohammedanism are the daughters of Judaism, and their vital parts are essentially Jewish, our religion will thus both directly and indirectly help to shape the religion of the future. We may furthermore maintain, — if this can add to our happiness, — that Judaism, on account of its flexibility and its rationalism, will flow with greater ease than any other of the present religious systems into the religion of the future, and thus become its mainstay.

With these explanations I should like to close my researches; but I cannot dismiss the subject without answering one more question, which has frequently been asked of late by my hearers, both Jews and Gentiles, — the question, What is Judaism? It would take another course, of at least ten lectures, should I endeavor to solve this question otherwise than metaphorically. You must, therefore, be satisfied with a figurative explanation.

Fables tell of a bird, of great beauty, which is so rare that only one specimen of its race exists on earth, and which is neither male nor female. The Phœnix is said to live to a very old age; but when he feels that death is near, he lines his nest with all kinds of odorous plants, sets fire to it, and burns himself with it. Out of the ashes, however, rises a new bird, young, vigorous, and still more beautiful than was his ancestor.

Judaism is such a phœnix. It is the *constantly changing but ever living religion of humanity.*

Whenever it feels that a change is needed, that its body has outlived its usefulness, it sets fire to its earthly environment; and, purified by the flames, it rises from the ashes in a new guise, but chanting the same old song, —

There is but one God, and all human beings are brethren.

NOTE.

It is quite natural and therefore pardonable in a reader of these ten lectures to ask the following questions : —

1. Does the author represent therein what *all* Israelites think of the Bible, of the Messiah, and of the hope in a return to Palestine?

2. If not, does he voice the opinion of at least a small number of Israelites? or

3. Does he stand all alone by himself and unsupported by any of his brethren, merely expressing his own individual views on these topics?

The author most decidedly disclaims to speak in behalf of all Israelites collectively; though he feels confident that most of his views are shared by all intelligent American Israelites. To ascertan their number would be a rather difficult task, because cultured people, as a rule, do not make a public display of their religious opinions.

Supposing, however, that the number of his supporters is a small one, that they form only an infinitesimal fraction of the whole Jewish population, what does it matter? Does not one intelligent, cultured person who sides with him more than outbalance a host of unintelligent, unlearned, and superstitious people who may rise in opposition to his declarations?

As a proof, merely, that he does not stand entirely alone and unsupported, he has added the following two lectures to the previous ten, from which the reader will learn that not an inconsiderable number of rabbies, who are renowned both for their profound scholarship and their high moral character, and who officiate in the largest and most celebrated Jewish congregations in America, have recently agreed upon a platform of principles every plank of which tallies exactly with the views expressed by the author.

The two lectures on "The Pittsburg Conference" will, therefore, prove interesting reading, and speak for themselves.

XI.

THE PITTSBURG CONFERENCE: ITS CAUSES.

UPON the urgent solicitation of the Rev. Dr. Kohler, of New York city, about sixteen rabbies, all belonging to the reformed wing of Judaism, assembled four weeks ago in Pittsburg, Penn.; and after a lively debate, they passed, without one dissenting vote, a set of resolutions which they termed a declaration of principles.

The learned gentlemen had come to the meeting of their own free will and accord; they had paid their own expenses: they had not been sent by their congregations or by any other body of Israelites to represent their views, and their utterances were therefore the utterances of private individuals, who could claim no other authority for them save that which sound judgment, intelligently and sincerely exercised, always carries with it.

The proceedings of the meeting were spread with electric rapidity all over the country; and the principles declared by them are now running the gauntlet of public criticism.

It matters little in what proportion the number of rabbies who assembled in Pittsburg stands to the number of Jewish congregations in America: it matters little whether these gentlemen voice the sentiment of the members of their several congregations: it matters little whether they are old or young, or whether they come from the East or the West; their declaration of principles is entitled to the attention of every intelligent American Israelite.

Whenever a number of men, in open assembly, boldly assert an opinion which runs counter to current ideas, but which impresses us with the sincerity of their purpose and the purity of their motives, we are in duty bound to give them a hearing. Experience ought to have taught us that a new truth never was championed by the many, but by the few, and that the great number of devotees is not always a true criterion of the worthiness of a cause. We ought to have learned by this time to be the more careful about condemning a measure the greater the opposition is which rises against it. The very greatness of that opposition is the best proof that something of vast importance must be hidden in the measure, calling for it. Men do not use heavy artillery to demolish houses built of cards. The bomb-shells which so far have been fired at the results of the conference, by the orthodox press or by over-zealous pulpit orators, are sufficient proof that the principles declared at Pittsburg are not made of pasteboard, but of solid masonry.

An assembly of sixteen intelligent men, who are all highly educated and well versed in the history of Judaism; who all have made theology the study of their lives; who all are supposed to represent the views held by the most prominent congregations of America, — such an assembly, be it authorized or unauthorized, carries some weight at least with it. The views which these gentlemen so freely expressed in their declaration of principles ought, therefore, to be studied by every conscientious Israelite, and neither be judged in an angry mood nor condemned in haste.

Although personally I am ready to subscribe to every paragraph of the Pittsburg platform, and although I feel now extremely sorry that circumstances over which I had no control prevented me from being present at that momentous meeting, I do not wish you to be biassed in your decision by me or anybody else, nor to look at only one side of the shield.

It becomes my duty to lay the whole matter before you, and to discuss it with all possible impartiality; but it is as well your duty to grant to such an important matter some of your leisure time, to think about it, and to discuss it in the circles of your friends. If you should become convinced of the timeliness and the soundness of the principles declared by the conference, you ought to ratify them, to strengthen the cause morally by your approval, and to encourage the bold leaders of the movement by your acclamation: if, on the other hand, you should detect the least fallacy, the least inconsistency, in them, you ought to denounce them openly; but we should both grossly neglect our duty, you as members of this congregation and I as its leader, should we pass with indifference or in silence over a measure which cuts so deeply into the flesh, and to the very bone of what some call Judaism; and which may in course of time revolutionize the whole structure of our religion.

It may appear to many that the Pittsburg Conference and the subsequent declaration of principles was an unnecessary movement, premature, and entirely uncalled-for. Nobody had invited these rabbies, or urged them to formulate their platform: apparently, there was no reason whatsoever for their meeting, or for their agressive policy: apparently, in the very midst of peace they have raised the battle-cry, and have fired the first shot over the peacefully slumbering Jewish communities. Apparently, the platform resolved upon is a novelty, which is expected to produce a desirable effect.

But the Pittsburg Conference is not a cause,

which is to produce an effect: on the contrary, it is an effect, which had been produced by a cause. It is not an uncalled-for measure: on the contrary, the members of the conference were forced into it by the pressure of their consciences. The hypocrisy and inconsistency of the present state of religious affairs had become too great for them to be borne any longer. For years the most prominent of these gentlemen had in vain endeavored to reconcile the past with the present, to patch up the outworn religious garment, and to fit it to a body which had outgrown it. No sooner had they stretched it on the one side when it shrank on the other: no sooner had they mended it in one place when it burst open somewhere else. They finally came to the conclusion that a new garment was needed; and therefore they cast away the old shreds.

A flash of lightning is the discharge of a quantity of electricity which has been accumulating in the clouds for some time: thus is the Pittsburg Conference merely a discharge of new thought which had been silently growing and ripening in the minds of people during the last fifty years.

Before, therefore, we enter upon a discussion of the actual work of the conference, before we take up the declaration of principles in paragraphical order, I consider it of the greatest importance to acquaint you with the causes which have produced such an astonishing result, and to disclose to you a few glimpses of the history of American Judaism; a history which is yet too young to have found a historian.

Every species of plant is subdivided into families, which, though they are alike in their main features, differ from one another in minor points. This difference in the size of the foliage, in the color and the odor of the blossom, is sometimes caused by climatic influences. The same law of nature prevails in the animal kingdom. A similar one holds good in the realms of thought and religion. The highest productions of the human mind are not exempt from it. Every religion is influenced not only by the political and social condition of its adherents, but by the very climate in which it lives. The very same religion assumes a different form in different countries. Both Catholicism and Protestantism have a far different appearance in northern and southern countries; upon European and upon American soil.

This law of nature once known and qualified, it will be easily understood why Judaism has been divided into so many families; why the Portuguese Jew differs so widely from the German, the German again from the Polish, English, or Dutch Jew. It will be easily understood to be quite natural that a new kind of

Judaism must spring up upon American soil, which, though it may carry all the marks of the species, may still differ widely from the other families in its structure.

The seed of Judaism which had been brought across the ocean to the shores of this continent found a soil here far different from that upon which it had been accustomed to grow. Take a plant which you have kept in a vase of sand and in a dark cellar, and transfer it to the fertile ground of a garden, where light and air and moisture are to be had in abundance; and you will soon observe a marked change in its structure and foliage; and after a few generations it will differ widely from its prototype.

The time when Judaism was transplanted to American soil will in the future be considered a turning-point in its history. At the most favorable periods of its existence it had never been more than a tolerated creed. In the most enlightened and humane countries of Europe, Asia, and Africa, our ancestors had been only tolerated; and it had been only tolerance for which they had dared to beg. In no country of the world have they ever been embraced by the general legislation: from the time of the Roman Cæsars to this very day they have stood under separate laws, which were extended, contracted, or annulled, according to the favor or disfavor which they found in the eye of the ruler. America is the first country which has no such word as tolerance in its political dictionary. It is the first country which has practically severed the connection between church and state, and which acknowledges no denominational differences before its laws. The codes of this country ignore every distinction of race and creed, and thus place the Israelite upon a level with his fellow-citizens.

As a plant which has been kept in the darkness of a cellar straightens its stem and spreads its foliage when transplanted into a sunny garden, thus the Israelite, as soon as the free air of America fanned his face, and the sunlight of liberty warmed his stiffened limbs, lifted up his head, which he had been compelled to bend submissively in Europe. He stretched himself to the full extent of his growth, and accustomed himself to his new surroundings. Unhampered by adverse legislation, he soon succeeded in establishing for himself and his dear ones a comfortable home in the land of his adoption; and by his honesty, his industry, and his temperate habits, he won in general for himself the respect of his fellow-citizens.

His spiritual progress, however, his advancement in religion, did not keep pace with his outward prosperity; it was perhaps retarded on account of it. In the old country he had been compelled by the state or by common usage to belong to some religious community. He had become accustomed there to let others think for him; and if he had ever dared to hold a view of his own, he would have been afraid to express it. Upon American soil all this was changed. No pressure whatever would force him to join a religious community. It was left to his own free will to associate with whomever he pleased. He had, furthermore, the right, not only to think for himself, but to speak out his opinion. He learned to argue a point, and to submit only to better judgment. Rationalistic tendencies, which are the inheritance of every Israelite, developed rapidly under the favorable conditions which were granted to him upon American soil.

This freedom, as I said, became dangerous to his religious advancement. Like a schoolboy in vacation, he did not know what to do with himself; there was no authority which he would or could respect. He did not yet understand the true mission of congregational life; he did not yet see how great a power of morality and respectability a religious union is. He was not yet aware that if he desired to rise in the estimation of his fellow-citizens he must be represented before them also in his higher aspirations. In the hurly-burly of a busy life he lost sight of religion, and kept aloof from all religious affairs. And, after all, what had religion been to him before? Nothing but a bundle of forms, a fardel, which he threw from his shoulders as soon as the power which compelled him to carry it had lost its grip upon him.

Some of these forms, however, though burdensome, had become dear to him by long custom; there were some rites which he considered necessary to his well-being. He observed the table laws as well as he could; he had the Abrahamitic rite performed on his children whenever it was possible; and, no matter how he had lived, or with whom he had associated during his lifetime, some superstitious fear made it desirable for him to be buried amongst his brethren, in a Jewish burial-ground. It was for the sake of maintaining a graveyard, and not for the sake of moral elevation, that the first Jewish congregations were formed in America. Our congregational life, indeed, was born upon burial-places; most of our proud temples have been' erected upon graveyards. No wonder, therefore, that the stillness of death hovers over them.

When public worship was added to the inducements which a congregation held out to the member, the spirit of freedom became a new obstacle to the development of our religion. The different elements which had gathered here from all parts of the world could not agree with one another. Every one had brought a certain usage from home to which he had been accustomed; and this Minhag, as he called it, he would never give up. In the old country he could be compelled to adopt the ritual sanctioned by the state or by rabbinical authority; but what in the world could compel him here in this free country to give up any of his fancies? If the congregation would not suit him, he would simply resign and start a new one which would be more pliable. It may be ludicrous to speak of race distinctions in a people which has preserved the purity of its blood with such great care as the Jews have; but, all the same, there it was. The German, Polish, Dutch, and English Jews could not agree with one another; they were prejudiced, — I cannot tell by what, — against one another, and they carried their distrust even into religion. They split, therefore, into numerous small congregations, none of which was able to support itself decently, or to show efficient work; none of which would give up one iota of its whims and join the next one in a body.

Now, what did the Jewish clergy do during all this time? There was none. In a country where the President holds office for only four years, and where the power of high state or city officials is limited to one year, the rabbi, no matter how learned and conscientious, could win no influence over his people. He was the paid official, who had to fulfil certain duties defined in a written contract. It was his first duty to please the secular leaders of the congregation. He had to carry out their wishes; and any opposition to them was tantamount to his dismissal. Fifty years ago there was no Jewish clergy to speak of in this country. All these conditions, however, changed. The emigration, which since the year 1848 has increased with every year, brought an energetic younger element to these shores; and a new generation had in the meantime arisen in this country, which had passed through the amalgamating process of our public schools; and these two elements found allies in each other. American Judaism began to speak. A Jewish press made its appearance; and, though its struggles were hard, it succeeded in spreading enlightenment and in removing somewhat the impediment of race prejudice.

The lack of pressure from without was made good by the urgent demand from within for centralization. Orders and societies for all kinds of purposes sprang up, around which the straying elements gathered, and by means of which they became disciplined. The congregations profited by the general activity; and the reform movement imported from Germany now found a warm reception, and exactly the ground which it needed for its development.

Although the opposition to reform had been very powerful, and had seemed to be almost invincible, the liberal movement carried the day; and the most orthodox of American congregations seems radically reformed if compared with similar congregations in Europe. The clergy which filled the pulpits of the reformed denomination worked itself step by step into recognition. Its conscientiousness, its learning, its earnest will, its ability, made an everlasting impression upon the laity; and thus the influence of the Jewish rabbi upon the formation of American Judaism was somewhat increased.

However, the whole structure of reform which, had arisen so suddenly under the impulse of the moment had been built upon sand. It lacked a foundation; it lacked principle. Reform had so far been a compromise between the past and the present, and had, therefore, given satisfaction to neither party. Reform had so far changed the outward appearance of our religion; it had so far removed nothing but ceremonies which had outlived their usefulness; but it had never touched the root; it had never attempted to examine whether or not some of the underlying principles had become obsolete.

On the one hand, modern researches, modern science, and modern philosophy, had revolutionized the world; they had thrown a searching light upon the history of mankind; and by this light a great many errors were discovered which formerly had been covered by the night of ignorance. All religious denominations had been compelled to change their front, and Judaism, rational and flexible as it is, could not remain in the rear. On the other hand, customs and usages which had lived for thousands of years are not so easily thrown aside; even if we become convinced of their uselessness, we revere them as relics, and dislike to part with them.

This anomaly soon became evident. Congregational life retrograded on account of it. The most gorgeous temples, the most artistic music, and the most elaborate sermons, failed to attract an audience. There was a discrepancy between the official sermon of the rabbi and his private utterances; there was a discrepancy between the teachings of the temple and the practices of the home. This inconsistency created hypocrisy, and alienated the most intelligent part of the Jewish population from religion.

For want of a platform upon which an intelligent man could build up his religion, many turned away from Judaism and joined the ranks of the atheists. The fervor with which American Jews hailed the establishment of a society for ethical culture, gave evidence, on the one hand, of a strong and warm religious sentiment; on the other, of the dissatisfaction of the thinking part of the Jewish population with the patchwork of reform.

A definition of what modern Judaism is, was needed. It became evident that we must cut loose from the sinking ship, or be drowned with it.

Impressed with the urgency of the demand for a new platform, for a definition which should finally establish a basis for our future development, the gentlemen who assembled at Pittsburg rose to the emergency. They spoke out simultaneously what they had harbored for years in their hearts, but had not dared to utter. They defined modern Judaism and opened the way for its progress. Without losing the connection with the past, they made Judaism the religion of the future. Upon the Pittsburg Platform every intelligent man can stand without the fear of breaking through it. It stands elevated above superstition, and will never be reached by the waves of atheism.

The change which Judaism by necessity had to undergo upon the new soil has now been accomplished. American Judaism has now passed its first stage; and the Declaration of Principles laid down by the conference is the seed from which a new plant will grow, which, though differing in structure, foliage, and color, from the European family, will still bear the marks of the same species.

The Pittsburg Conference was the natural outcome of years of religious indifference and stagnation: it was the reconciliation of modern thought with religious sentiment: it was the proof of the immortality of Judaism. It was rather the closing scene of a past period than the opening scene of a new one.

The bristling caterpillar and the gold-winged butterfly are one and the same insect, though they differ widely in their form and mode of living. The caterpillar, preparing its own coffin, transforms itself therein into the new creation. When its transformation is perfected, the butterfly bursts the cocoon and unfolds its wings, forcing its way into liberty, into the balmy air, to play with sunshine and flowers.

The Pittsburg Conference marks in like wise the bursting of the old and outgrown bonds of Judaism, and the emergence therefrom of its new and nobler phase.

XII.

THE PITTSBURG CONFERENCE: ITS WORK.

IN my last lecture I discussed the causes which in my opinion led to the Pittsburg Rabbinical Conference. Speaking now of its work, I know of no better introduction than to give the platform which has been constructed by the rabbies who formed that memorable conclave. The following is its full text:

In view of the wide divergence of conflicting ideas of Judaism to-day, we, as representatives of Reform Judaism in America, in continuation of the work begun in Philadelphia in 1869, unite upon the following principles:—

I. We recognize in every religion an attempt to grasp the infinite; and in every mode, source, or book of revelation held sacred in any religious system the consciousness of the indwelling of God in man. We hold that Judaism presents the highest conception of the God idea as taught in our Scriptures and developed and spiritualized by the Jewish teachers in accordance with the moral and philosophical progress of their respective ages. We maintain that Judaism preserved and defended, amid continual struggles and trials, under enforced isolation, the God idea as the central truth for the whole human race.

II. We recognize in the Bible the record of the conservation of the Jewish people to its mission as priest of the one God, and value it as the most potent instrument of religious and moral instruction. We hold that the modern discoveries and scientific researches in the domain of nature and history are *not* antagonistic to the doctrines of Judaism; the Bible reflecting the primitive ideas of its own age, and at times clothing its conceptions of divine providence and justice dealing with man in miraculous narratives.

III. We recognize in the Mosaic legislation a system of training the Jewish people for its mission during its national life in Palestine; and to-day we accept as binding only the moral laws, and maintain only such ceremonies as elevate and sanctify our lives, but reject all such as are not adapted to the views and habits of modern civilization.

IV. We hold that all such Mosaic and rabbinical laws as regulated diet, priestly purity, and dress, originated in ages and under the influence of ideas altogether foreign to our present mental and spiritual state. They fail to impress the modern Jew with a spirit of priestly holiness; and their observance in our days is apt rather to obstruct than to further modern spiritual elevation.

V. We recognize in the modern era of universal culture of heart and intellect the approach to the realization of Israel's great Messianic hope for the establishment of the kingdom of truth, justice, and peace, amongst all men. We consider ourselves no longer a nation, but a religious community; and therefore expect neither a return to Palestine, nor a sacrificial worship under the sons of Aaron, nor the restoration of the laws concerning the Jewish state.

VI. We recognize in Judaism a progressive religion, ever striving to be in accord with the postulates of reason. We are convinced of the utmost necessity of preserving the historical identity with our great past. Christianity and Islam being daughter religions of Judaism, we appreciate their providential mission to and in the spreading of monotheistic and moral truth. We acknowledge that the spirit of broad humanity of our age is our ally in the fulfilment of our mission; and therefore we extend the hand of fellowship to all who operate with us in the establishment of the reign of truth and righteousness among men.

VII. We re-assert the doctrine of Judaism, that the soul of man is immortal: grounding this belief on the divine nature of the human spirit, which forever finds bliss in righteousness and misery in wickedness. We reject, as ideas not rooted in Judaism, the beliefs both in bodily resurrection and in Gehenna and Eden (Hell and Paradise) as abodes for everlasting punishment or reward.

VIII. In full accordance with the spirit of Mosaic legislation, which strives to regulate the relations between rich and poor, we deem it our duty to participate in the great task of modern times: to solve, on the basis of justice and righteousness, the problems produced by the contrasts and evils of the present organization of society.

A French statesman of the last century is credited with the paradox that the human language was invented for the sake of concealing one's thoughts, and that his remark must have been founded upon some sharp observation, and is not altogether absurd, is again substantiated by the eight paragraphs of the Pittsburg Platform. Indeed, the greater part of their phraseology is merely ornamental; and if it had not been for the purpose of concealing some thoughts, it would have been superfluous. But the task of the Convention was a difficult one. It was to speak the truth before a community unaccustomed to its sound, and unwilling to hear it. It became therefore necessary to sugar-coat the bitter pill which the patient was to take; and instead of criticising the verbosity of the eight paragraphs, let us simply do, what I suppose the framers wish us to do, remove the shell and lay bare the kernel.

It was quite natural that the first and most prominent plank in the platform of a religion must be a definition of the God idea. Unless a religion denies the existence of a God, it must give some approximate description of its conception of the supreme being. However, this very *conditio sine qua non* has once before led to a rupture and break-up of a rabbinical conference. Some of the divines composing it objected to the theory of a personal God; others to that of an impersonal divinity.

Guided by this sad experience, the Pittsburg Conference, though maintaining that the existence of a God stands above any doubt, refrained from defining the indefinable. It maintained, rightly, that religion is only an attempt to grasp the infinite; that all definitions of the supreme being which have come down to us so far by means of a so-called sacred literature are simply the proof of our consciousness of the indwelling of God in man. It furthermore maintained that Judaism has held the highest conception of God at every period of its existence; that it has developed and spiritualized it in accordance with the moral and philosophical progress of the successive ages.

If this first paragraph is to be translated into plainer language, it says no more and no less than that our conception of God has been the product of numerous evolutions; that the God of Moses was evolved from that of Abraham; that the God of Isaiah was an improvement over that of Samuel; and that consequently our conception of God to-day must be higher, grander, and purer, than that of past generations, in the same proportion as humanity has advanced morally and intellectually and its mental horizon has been extended. The theory of evolution adapted to the God idea places us far above our ancestors, and suggests the hope that future generations will come still nearer to its true conception. It furthermore grants to every individual the right of defining God as he pleases and is able to; and this is a concession which has never been made before, but which is the basis for a universal religion, for the religion of humanity. Let us understand this point well.

There are no two persons who hold exactly the same conception of the divinity. Their ideas may tally in some points; but they will differ in others. The greater the difference in their intellect and their education is, the greater and the more marked will be the difference between their Gods. Heretofore every religious system has had a well-defined God idea, the knowledge of which it claimed to have obtained by special revelation; and therefore it promulgated it as the only correct one, even at the point of the sword, and compelled its adherents, and, if possible, its opponents even, to submit to it and to acquiesce in it. Human reason, however, revolted against such compulsion. The God idea of Moses towered far above that of his contemporaries; still, he found it impossible to elevate his people to his ideas, and it took more than half a millennium before his conception of God had become popular. Just as impossible would it have been for the people to drag Moses down to their low standpoint.

Place a man of the stamp of an Emerson by the side of a man who, though he may be the most honest and conscientious of mortals, has not received a training in abstract thinking. Place two such men side by side, and demand of them to grasp the selfsame God idea. Although God, the Infinite, is the same being that he has been and shall ever be, although our conception of him does not change a particle of his essence, such a demand would be absurd. The one will follow the vestiges of God through the immensities of the spheres; he will see his grandeur in the turbulent waves of the history of mankind; he will detect his presence in his consciousness of self, and philosophically analyze his essence as it presents itself in the different departments of the human mind. The other will behold in him merely the giver of his daily bread and the stern judge of his actions; he will unburden his heart before him in prayer, and expect of *him*, his best and most powerful friend, that he will intercede in the trivial affairs of life; he will live and die in what he calls the fear of God. What right would the first one have to force his world-embracing ideas of God upon the second one? And by what right could the second one compel the first one to accept his anthropomorphic theories? All religious dissensions which have disunited the human brotherhood, all religious persecutions and wars which have soiled the record of humanity, had their origin in the belief that their own God idea alone was the correct one; that all others, being erroneous, were an insult to God, which the holders of the true idea must by right avenge.

But from the time that Lessing wrote his "Nathan the Wise," and in the fable of the three rings made him utter the remarkable words, "The genuine ring has perhaps been lost, and ye all three are deceived impostors (betrogene

Betrüger)," from that time a change of thought came over the world. Intelligent men allowed to others their own conceptions of God, but demanded the same privilege for themselves. Religious controversies disappeared, or lost their sting. The God idea of a man was tested by the way he realized it in his life. If it had the result of making him an honest man, it was called genuine, no matter how high or how low its standard was; if it contained no such force, it was rejected as wrong, no matter how scrupulously that man performed the ceremonies of his church, and how hypocritically he proclaimed his belief in God.

As intelligent men, we can no longer adhere to the theory that the God ideas of an Abraham, a Moses, or Isaiah, were the only correct ones; that the conception which our ancestors had of God is exclusively the only true one; that, to speak in the words of the fable, we alone own the genuine ring. Religion is for us, as the Conference grandly defines it, "an attempt merely to grasp the infinite;" and with every step which humanity has advanced, with every evolution through which the history of Israel has passed, these attempts have grown bolder and more successful. Led by the van of philosophers and thinkers of all nationalities, the great bulk of humanity has progressed, though slowly, in its religious views. The monotheistic God idea has won the victory, and has replaced polytheism and pantheism. The average conception of God has become purer and more sublime than it ever was before; and there is no doubt that it will receive its highest development and its loftiest spiritualization, provided full freedom is left to the individual mind to grasp the infinite to the extent of its compass. As the first of the Mosaic laws was a proclamation of freedom, so the first paragraph of the Pittsburg Convention removes the shackles of a uniform and unchangeable God idea, and claims the liberty for every man to form his own idea concerning the great Ehejeh asher Ehejeh; or, in other words, gives him full liberty in his attempts to grasp the infinite.

Upon this plank the intelligent of all sects and denominations can unite. It is a plank for the religion of the future.

The Conference found it necessary to devote several paragraphs to its definition of the Bible. The Bible is a book which has been in the possession of our nation for not less than twenty-three hundred years. Its old age alone makes it venerable to us; but it has a value for us besides its antiquity. It is an inexhaustible mine of wise and profound thought. Its pages are full of the noblest sentiment; its philosophy is comprehensive, its poetry soul-inspiring, its ethics both ennobling and practical. As a literary production, the Bible stands unsurpassed. If we had stopped right here, I believe that never a word would have been uttered against the venerable book. But we did not stop there. The Bible, probably on account of its sublimity, was pronounced to be the direct work of God. It was stated that God himself wrote, or at least dictated, every word of it; that he distinctly expressed his sovereign will by means of it; that, therefore, not one of the laws contained therein could be abrogated, changed, or abolished; that we may interpret its wording, but are not allowed to question one of its statements. The belief in the divinity of the Bible was made an article of creed. Down to the end of the last century, no religious system ever questioned the principle of revelation by means of a book; on the contrary, every religious system thought it to be a matter of utmost necessity to prove its genuineness by such a book. Christianity brought forth the New Testament to match and offset the old one; Mohammed produced the Koran; and even the present Mormonism attempted to prove its divine mission by documentary evidence.

The development of science, however, has undermined in the course of time the belief in the divinity of the Bible. As a book of human origin, reflecting the ideas of past generations and treasuring up the wisdom of humanity in a condensed form, common sense could revere the book; but it revolted against its alleged divine authorship. Grand as is the Bible when considered as the product of man, it reflects little honor upon a divine author. While the creations of God are all perfect, the Bible is imperfect. It requires a strong dose of credulity to cover its deficiencies and discrepancies. Science and modern research became, therefore, the most implacable enemies of the Bible; but not in so far as the Bible itself is concerned; in so far only as a divine authorship is claimed for it, and its errors are presented to us as undeniable truth on the strength of it.

All attempts to reconcile with modern thought the statements and narratives of the Bible taken literally have so far failed; and while on the one hand we were afraid to haul down the flag and accept the conditions of the victor, our daily life brought us on the other hand in conflict with and in constant divergence from both the historical part of the Bible and some of its laws. A shameless hypocrisy, which undermined all religious fervor, was the consequence of it. It became evident that this unnatural state of affairs was to be brought to an end unless the best and sincerest element were to be lost for religion. There were only two ways before us, one of which must be chosen: either the

Bible was the direct word of God, in which case every one of its prescriptions must be fulfilled by us, no matter whether it was appropriate or not; we had no right to change any of them either by way of interpretation or interpolation; if they were the laws of God, they must stand for all times and all countries. Or, the Bible was the product of human genius, in which case we could easily account for its deficiencies. We could easily comprehend that the writers, without the remotest idea of deceiving us, had explained things to the best of their knowledge; we could subtract poetical exaggeration and reduce facts to their possibly true basis; we could admire the legislation of the past, and accept of it what was useful and practicable for us; we could claim the right of legislating for ourselves as former generations did for themselves. Thus all antagonism against the Bible would cease at once, and it would become again the book of the world.

This bold step has been taken by the Pittsburg Conference. The doors have been thrown open to a normal progress of religion and to the development of new forms which will correspond better than the former with the demands of the hour, and will tend to elevate and sanctify our lives. The prevailing hypocrisy, the childish playing with antiquated forms which had been substituted for earnest, practical, religious work, have been done away with; and the principle, once boldly asserted and proclaimed, will soon give practical results.

It is with you to indorse or reject the definition of the Bible as given by the Pittsburg Conference. Your acceptance will open a new era in your religious life; it will cause you to determine for yourselves, and to work practically for religion; it will elevate you and sanctify your lives; it will make you zealous and enthusiastic in the service of a cause which will indeed be your cause. Your rejection of it would be tantamount to the former drugging indifference which has lulled all religion into sleep; it would mean empty churches, disorderly Sabbath-schools, discord between parents and children, moral weakness, and final extinction of morality.

These two points were the most important ones which came before the Conference. They rise above the trivialities of the Sabbath question and others of the same character. In fact, they include them. Freeing you from the slavery of the past, they give you the power of legislation, and leave it with you to adjust all religious forms in accordance with the dictates of your common sense and your conscience.

The other points are all of minor importance. These two points once understood, it becomes evident that we form no nationality, but a religious sect; that we reject all hopes in the advent of a personal Messiah; and, if the word "Messianic" is needed in the religious vocabulary, we express by it the hope in a time when all humanity will have reached its highest development. In the meantime, and this the eighth paragraph lays to our heart, we must not divorce religion from life; we must participate as a body in the solution of all the problems of the day; we must lend a helping hand, as a body, to the re-organization of society and to the removal of all the evils which the present system carries with it. We must participate, as a body, in the amelioration of the condition of our less fortunate brethren; and the work of charity must become one of the noblest branches of religious activity.

The hope of immortality, too, was inserted as a plank in the Pittsburg platform. Its existence was acknowledged; but no definition was attempted in a matter which defies definition. All those superstitious fancies which have crept into Judaism, as that of heaven and hell, have been rejected; the Conference has dealt with "one world at a time."

This has been the work of the Conference; and every intelligent Israelite can stand upon its platform, for it is truly Jewish in its spirit. It acknowledges the one God, the common

Father of mankind; it acknowledges the great services which Israel has rendered to humanity, in spreading the monotheistic idea; it proclaims liberty of thought; it appreciates in the Bible a literary treasure, venerable by its age, and admirable on account of the inexhaustible stores of wisdom which it contains; it makes us co-workers in the great work of humanity, and bids us to help build up the grand dome of human civilization; it inspires us with the hope of immortality, without exciting our sensuality or our fear.

As could not have been expected otherwise, this work has been furiously attacked. But by whom? By all such as could not or would not think; by all such as preferred indifference to active work; by all such as have been accustomed to look at one side of a question only; by all such as would profit by their hypocrisy, and lose materially if a new avenue were opened. An army, no matter how large, if recruited of a lazy, timid, and ignorant element, will be as easily put to flight by a small body of courageous men, as was the contingent which Falstaff led into the field.

I could close my discussion of the subject right here, were it not that the work of the Conference has been misrepresented by its foes; were it not that, ignoring its true inwardness, they have picked up two trifling points which had been mentioned informally only at the Conference in connection with the main principles, and attempted to scare all true Israelites from it. These two points are the Sabbath question and the performance of the Abrahamitic rite. Let us face these two questions fairly and squarely. There is a certain timidity observable as soon as they are touched upon even in private conversation; but if it is true that they are indeed the main pillars of Judaism, they ought to be strong enough to bear the light of a fair discussion at least. I fail to see why we should refrain from treating these points publicly: as the modern rabbi is no infallible Pope, and grants his hearers the privilege of differing from him.

In regard to the Sabbath, the Conference could not but acknowledge the historical Sabbath — our Sabbath; — but it warned against the customary hypocrisy of naming one day of rest and of keeping another, or none at all. The main principle of the Sabbath is not that we visit a temple and listen to a sermon; it is our actual abstinence from work. The divine worship on that day is a secondary consideration. Leaving the power of decision in your own hands, the Conference merely advised to adhere to a principle; that is, to rest from work, and consistently with it to call that day your Sabbath on which in reality you abstain from labor. The Sabbath has been instituted for the sake of man, not for the sake of God; and even if the latter were the case, what pleasure could the supreme being derive from your theoretical adherence to one day and practical observance of another or none. It was furthermore maintained that there is no reason why religious services should not be held on any day in the week in addition to the Sabbath service, and that therefore no objection could be raised if a congregation decide to meet on Sunday too. The prevailing hypocrisy, which wishes to work all seven days of the week, and therefore is more than pleased with the present shameful state of affairs, arose against the truthful and conscientious stand taken by the members of the conference in an informal debate.

The second point is the Abrahamitic rite; in regard to which Dr. Kohler of New York has alone expressed himself. Let us argue this point also. The sometimes dangerous operation can be justified by two reasons only. The one is that it is believed to be a token of the covenant made between God and Abraham; that it is firmly believed that the supreme being demanded the surgical and painful operation of Abraham. That such has indeed been the case is proven by no other evidence than the Bible. I have repeated it frequently that it is in vain to argue with one who wishes to believe. Before belief all arguments become powerless. The man, therefore, who has this operation performed on his child, because he believes firmly that God has made it the signature to a contract between himself and man — such a person is perfectly justified in his act before God and man. I shall always respect him for it.

But this standpoint has been given up long since. It appeared too absurd to think of God, the Infinite, demanding such an operation; the religious fort, the only tenable one, was evacuated, and the pious intrenched themselves behind another bulwark. They said it is a sanitary measure. They quoted medical authorities in favor of it: they claimed that not only had this operation been necessary in former ages, in a warmer climate, but that even to-day it is a preventive of diseases brought about by immorality.

Thus they build their arguments upon the basis that, as immorality was to be expected, the well-deserved punishment for it ought to be frustrated. This is their logic. I shall not speak now of numerous cases where children have died on account of the operation: on the contrary, I shall accept for a moment the standpoint of the defenders of the ceremony, namely the sanitary view of it. Vaccination is surely as much a preventive of a disease as can be claimed for circumcision. Vaccination prevents an epidemic which comes over the individual without his fault, and which in many cases results in death; while the Abrahamitic rite prevents diseases caused by immorality, and not easily resulting in death. But who would dream of making vaccination a religious rite of high importance? Who would claim that a person not vaccinated could not be admitted into a religious community, or that religion is in danger, if vaccination is neglected? If circumcision is merely a sanitary measure, what has it to do with religion? We must, then, grant liberty to every parent to do as he sees fit. If he chooses to have his child circumcised, why not? We should hold him responsible only that the infant be not harmed by an unskilled practitioner. If the parent should choose otherwise, why reject him or his children from religious intercourse with us? Either standpoint is weak. The whole ceremony is to-day but a matter of custom; and indifferrence or some superstitious fear makes parents allow it. Such customs die slowly; and we have no right to interfere with the conscience of anybody. Let everybody do as he pleases; but it behooves us to speak out the truth and to say that this usage has nothing to do with religion. This is much better than to play hide-and-seek behind intrenchments which have been demolished by the fire of logic.

Liberty is the first principle of Judaism. Liberty stood godmother at its cradle: liberty has nursed it, and every postulate of liberty is therefore Jewish and strictly Jewish. Grant liberty to all also in regard to these two points, and you need not be afraid of losing the firm ground of Judaism. I maintain that liberty and Judaism are identical.

NOTE.— No sooner had the preceding twelve lectures been delivered, and abstracts of them published in the daily papers, than the author was importuned by numerous letters, pouring upon him from all parts of the country, to express himself more fully in regard to his version of what modern Judaism is, as well as in regard to some other theological questions which the writers made free to ask.

At that time, the author found it an absolutely impossible task to answer every one of these letters; but, in order to give to his correspondents some satisfaction at least, he has now added to this book, and for their special benefit, the following five lectures (previously delivered by him at different occasions), in which they will find not only all the information which they desire, but also the answers to their very queries.

XIII.

MODERN JUDAISM.

THE universe is a book of riddles, which God seems to have presented to humanity in order to keep it busy, and mankind indeed has ever busied itself in solving them one after another. No sooner had it deciphered one of the problems contained therein than it would joyfully clap its hands in a childlike manner and look proudly around as if to say: Now, am I not a clever fellow? and with new energy and without a moment's rest it would turn to the next enigma.

The more of these riddles will be solved, the higher will the standard of human civilization rise, and not until a solution shall have been found for the last problem: not until the last law of nature shall have been discovered, will humanity come to rest and to peace with itself.

It is indeed both gratifying and encouraging to peruse the many pagefuls of riddles which mankind has deciphered so far; it is a pleasure to read all the answers so carefully marked with indelible ink under every one of these problems, which before have puzzled the human mind; but must we not be astonished the more when we find that one riddle which occurs in an endless variety, on almost every page, has been left without an answer? How has this happened? How could it have happened? Has this one riddle been overlooked, or has it been intentionally disregarded?

For three thousand years a nation has been living upon earth; it has lived and prospered in every zone, it has associated with every nation; its life has been open to research, but even to-day, as three thousand years ago, this nation has still remained a mystery to the world. To-day, as three thousand years ago, the Jew is an unsolved riddle to friend and foe, the mystery of his existence has never been cleared up, the secret of his endurance has never been divulged, the importance of his mission has never been understood.

When Abraham, the first of the Hebrews, appeared in Canaan, he was a riddle to the people of that country. They transacted business with him, they allied themselves to him in peace and war; but they never understood him. The ancient Egyptians never understood the children of Israel, who are said to have sojourned amongst them for more than three hundred years. The Jew was a mystery to the Persians, the Greeks, and the Romans, and he has remained to be an unsolved riddle even to all the modern nations to this very day. Our enlightened contemporaries do not know us; they have no measurement for our character; they are ignorant of our best qualities; they do not know how we live, how we act, how we feel. They know nothing of our true sentiments, of our predilections, of our hopes and aspirations. They gauge the nation by the individual with whom chance brings them in contact. Whenever they find a noble specimen of our race, they imagine that all the rest is like it : whenever their acquaintance is low-bred, they think that the rest is no better than he. There stands the Jew, with his grand history, with his immense literature, still an enigma, an interrogation point in human society.

There has never been an author or an actor who has been able to represent the Jew as he is. They either lionized and idealized him, or made a caricature of him. Neither Shakespeare's Shylock nor Dickens' Fagin is a true representation of a Jew — nor is Lessing's Nathan. They all are creations of fancy, to which never a true prototype was found amongst our race.

The very same mystery enshrouds our religion. Judaism, too, is a riddle to the world. It impressed Malchizedeck with the same awe as it did afterwards Darius, Alexander the

Great, and the Roman Cæsars. It gave birth to the religions of to-day, to Christianity and to Islam; but these children were never able to comprehend their mother. They gazed at her with awe, but even at their most advanced age they failed to understand her stern grandeur. There it stands after an existence of three thousand years, after a continuous struggle of three thousand years, still as youthful and vigorous as ever, but still the same mystery to the world as before.

It is not mere phraseology, and by no means an empty oratorical turn, when I say that Judaism is still to-day an unsolved riddle, that even in our enlightened age it is as unknown to the world as it was in the dark ages of antiquity. One illustration will prove it.

Our friend, the Rev. Minot J. Savage, a gentleman, as you all know, combining profundity of thought with rare eloquence, who is renowned both for his deep scholarship and for the liberality of his views, lately addressed his congregation on the question, "Which religion is fitted to survive?" In a masterly exposé he willingly conceded that it is not Christianity which will survive. "It is not the most beautiful flower," he said in his introduction, "it is not the most valuable grass, it is not that which is of the most possible service to man, it is not that which is ideally best from man's standpoint, which of necessity survives. The fittest here means at its best that which is best fitted to its condition. In religion it is that theory which is best adapted to the advancement of the people that will survive." Then he maintained that all the different religions, Christianity included, will evolve and advance side by side, that they all will cast off their crude forms, their superstitions, their fallacies, and thus finally blend into that one religion which will survive as the fittest of all. It was well said. The same old Jewish doctrine of the Messianic time, of a time when all nations will acknowledge and adore the same God, was brought forth with full strength though in a modern garb — but not with a single word did the orator refer to the one religion which apparently always has been best fitted to its condition; not with a single word did he refer to that theory which has always been best adapted to the advancement of the people. He had not a single word for the religion which for three thousand years has withstood the pressure of time, the ill-will, yea, the persecution, of all the nations of the world, and which for three thousand years has constantly been casting off one crude form, one superstition, one fallacy, after another, without changing its principle. He had not a single word for Judaism. And why not? Because he does not know it, a fact for which we must not think less of him, nor hold him responsible. Judaism is a mystery, and no one outside its pale has ever been able to comprehend it. He shares his lack of knowledge of Judaism with the rest of mankind.

A still greater mystery surrounds what we now call "Modern Judaism." It is a term which defies interpretation. Modern Judaism is still less known to our Christian friends than ancient Judaism; the most liberal, the most advanced, the most erudite of our contemporaries do not know what to make of modern Judaism. One thinks it is an approach to Christianity, another claims that it is the death-rattle of Judaism, and a third that it is a transition to atheism. And not one of these versions is correct.

Even to our own people modern Judaism is a term the meaning of which is beclouded. Even the Jews of to-day do not know what to make of it, and we meet generally with the most absurd conceptions of it. To many it seems as if modern Judaism has no essentials, no consistency whatever, and is a trifling and playing with outward forms merely. They think that an organ and choir, the uncovered head, the abolition of the ancient prayer-book, and a Sunday-Sabbath are the sole requirements of modern Judaism; they feel attracted or repelled by it in the measure in which their personal inclinations favor indifferentism or sensationalism. But they too are mistaken.

I think the mystery begins with the adjective "modern." We speak of modern improvements, and mean by them all those contrivances which have been invented during the last few years to save time and labor, to make our surroundings more comfortable and pleasant; we speak of modern languages, and mean by them all those languages which at present are spoken by civilized nations. We speak of modern sciences, and mean by the term all those branches of knowledge which lately have risen into prominence. In one word, the term modern implies something that is new, and is always used in opposition to the term ancient.

But "modern" does not qualify Judaism in this sense. Modern Judaism is not a new kind of Judaism lately invented. Judaism has always been modern; Judaism always has been in advance of its time.

When Abraham entered Canaan and proclaimed the El Shaddai, his religion was surely a modern one. When Moses appeared before the people of Israel proclaiming the great I AM, his religion was modern Judaism. When King Solomon built and endowed the temple, and assumed duties which formerly had been the privilege of the priesthood, his Judaism was modern Judaism. When the prophets thundered against the custom of offering sacrifices, their religion surely was the modern Judaism of their age; when Ezra introduced the reading of the law, and when Rabbi Jochanan ben Saccai, after the destruction of the temple, substituted prayers for sacrifices, they were by all means the advocates of modern Judaism. In fact, Judaism has changed with every generation, and consequently has always been, so to say, modern.

The advocates of free religion claim that all the religions of the world are honest efforts on the part of men groping in darkness to find the secret of this life and the knowledge of all that pertains to God. But if this be true, we could as well begin to build a house from the roof downwards. The knowledge of God and the disclosure of the secret of life is the beginning and not the end of religion; Judaism therefore begins with the proposition that there is a God, it starts with disclosing the whole secret of existence, which is to love God above all, and our neighbor as ourselves, and, while walking in the pure sunlight of this fact, it dispels, step by step, degree by degree, the darkness which overshadows the world. Judaism has therefore been the only religion which could cast off one garment after another, which could adapt itself to the customs, the usages and opinions of each century, which could absorb every new philosophy and accommodate itself to every new theory without harming or endangering its essentials. All the other religions lost their identity as soon as they came in contact with a new truth, and each of their sects was split in two as soon as a difference of opinion arose between them. Judaism always remained intact; in Persia it became Persian, in Greece Grecian, in Italy Roman, in Germany German, in Russia Russian, and here it has become American, but it remained everywhere strictly Judaism. Thousands of years ago it absorbed with the same ease the philosophy of Aristotle as to-day it absorbs the theories of Darwin and Huxley. It remained always the same ancient, or, better, the same modern Judaism.

Our modern Judaism is not more or less than the adaptation of Judaism to the present age, to the present mode of living, to the present standard of knowledge. If all our institutions, our social and political order were to-day in a settled shape, we should find that modern Judaism too would appear in a more finished condition, and we should be better enabled to give a clear conception of it. But the social and political order of things is at present in a state of fermentation, the period in which we live is characterized by its chaotic aspect; and floating upon such unstable times modern Judaism sometimes appears to us rather shaky.

The invention and introduction of steam and electric power has changed not only the former order of things, but also the surface, the geography, the history, even the philosophy, of the world, in such a degree that humanity has not yet been able to keep step with it. A new order of things is preparing, old landmarks are changing, powers small and unnoticed before are rising into prominence, while others are on the decline. The struggle between labor and capital enters every day into new phases, communism and nihilism cannot any longer be talked out of existence; in a word, the whole world is becoming upset and revolutionized. The old house threatens to fall to pieces, and the new house is not yet ready. The world seems to be in labor pains, and still the hour for the birth of a new order has not yet struck.

How can it be expected that Judaism shall find its proper form under such circumstances? As a magnetic needle is not expected to stand still during a storm, but gives satisfaction when, though trembling from right to left, it again returns for a moment to its true position pointing northward, thus Judaism, though moving at present between extremes, still points out the right way. When the storm shall have subsided, when the waves shall have been smoothed down, Judaism will be found again in its proper place and in a more settled shape — the only religion fitted to survive.

Speaking of modern Judaism we must carefully distinguish between those forms which are the mere garment of religion, and those which pertain to its body. The soul of religion is still a creation for itself. Every religion has a soul, a body, and a vestment for this body. Judaism too has such a body, and this body was never found in want of a garment. But in a religion destined to survive, not only the garment is cast off from time to time, but the body itself changes, as the human body does from year to year. In the measure as the body expands the garment must be made larger. All those ceremonies which usually, but wrongly, are taken for the embodiment of a religion are its garment only, and adjust themselves from time to time to the body proper. Of Judaism both the soul and the body are immortal; the soul remains unchangeable, the body assumes from time to time different forms, the garment alone is allowed to wear away and to be replaced by a new one. The whole temple service, with priests and sacrifices, with breast-plates and altars, has been a mere cloak to cover the body of Judaism in its youth.

This body was the anthropology of that early age. God was represented as the king of the universe, and although no visible image of the deity was tolerated, the human mind of that time was unable to form a higher conception of the Almighty. With the dawn of a better and higher conception the body expanded, the garment fell away, and the measurement for a new suit of clothes had to be taken.

The researches of the last century have again so vastly changed the body of our religion that a new garment is in demand. This garment is not yet ready, it is making ; and as soon as the proportions of the new body shall be understood, and a correct measure of them shall have been taken, the new cloak will be finished at once. The present discord in regard to ceremonies, the present experimenting with all kinds of formulas, the feeling of discomfort which as a consequence pervades at present our religious life, are caused by the late expansion of the body of our religion and our desire to cover the bare places. We may for a time attempt to patch the old garment wherever it tears, but it is a poor policy, — love's labor lost. A new one is needed.

As I cannot define what modern Judaism is, I will at least direct your attention to some great changes which have expanded the body of Judaism and have therefore caused the demand for a new garb.

One is the change of opinion in regard to the origin of the Bible. For centuries the belief had been current, and seemed to have been the backbone of our religion, that the Bible was the direct word of God, that he had dictated every word literally to the authors of the different books, and that consequently no error or mistake could have occurred therein. If a passage would not agree with our common sense, we would spare no trouble to interpret it so as to make it fit. If our efforts were unsuccessful, we would simply bewail human blindness and our inability to see the true light, but we would never harbor the least doubt as to the literal truth of the Bible.

All our ceremonies, therefore, adapted themselves to this body. The reading and expounding of the law became the centre of the divine service. The very place in which the scroll of the law was kept, the very parchment upon which it was written, were held sacred. When a fire occurred in a synagogue, people would risk their lives to save the scrolls; not because it was a great expense to them to obtain new ones, but because they were considered holy. The preacher would discuss dark passages contained therein, and the text quoted from the good book was used by him as a foundation for his arguments. No human power could shake that evidence, and from it there was no appeal.

This belief has now vanished. The body of Judaism has assumed an entirely different form. We believe to-day that, in a certain degree, all literature is inspired by the divine being. We know that no author could write a line unless under divine inspiration. All that we call invention, discovery, progress, advancement, is a revelation. The new idea which flashes upon the mind of a great thinker, of an inventor or discoverer, the light which he perceives, while the rest of humanity does not yet see it, is a revelation of God. God speaks to men to-day as he has spoken before to them; he speaks louder and more distinct to the one than to the other, but he speaks always in the language of their time, in order to be understood by them. The truth of a revelation remains the same, though the wording of it may become erroneous on account of the medium through which it has to pass.

Thus the Bible is an inspired book, but not more inspired than any other. To us, it is, besides, a literary treasure accumulated by our nation, showing us how it has been evolved from its earliest days to the time when the last edition was revised. It is sacred to us on account of its antiquity, on account of the grand ideas expressed therein; but it has ceased to be infallible. We have ceased to cling to its letter, though we accept its spirit. All that is true in it we adopt; all that is erroneous we discard. We do not say any longer that a fact is true because it is recorded in the Bible; but we claim that a great many facts have been embodied in that book because they were thought to be true.

We know to-day that the five books of Moses were written several hundred years after Moses, not by one but by several authors; that they were written in a different order; that they were re-edited and revised. Concerning the other books, we know still less, — even the names of their authors may be fictitious.

On account of this change in the body of our religion, our present ceremonial will not fit any longer. The whole system of our public worship has ceased to give satisfaction on account of it. A new garment is making. A hundred years from now our ceremonies will have been changed to fit the new condition of things. If we should live to see that time, we should possibly feel quite uncomfortable; we should possibly not call the new creation Judaism; but Judaism it will be as long as the soul remains intact, which is, "Hear, Israel, the Lord thy God is one God."

Islam could not survive the destruction of the Koran. Christianity totters to-day on account of the blows which liberal thinkers direct against the divinity of the New and Old Testament, and it will soon fall, as all the liberals concede, on account of having no other foundation but the one; but Judaism will exist forever, even if its Bible shall be placed on the shelf with other books of the same grandeur or value. The structure of Judaism does not rest upon the Bible. Judaism existed before a letter of the Bible was written. Israel's mission is indeed not written upon combustible parchment and with a perishable pen; it is written with the finger of God, upon the indestructible pages of human history.

Long before the authority of the Bible had been shaken, that of the Talmud had vanished away. The Talmud is a work of great historical value. With its commentaries it is the petrified life of our nation during more than a thousand years. It is difficult to give a correct description of what the Talmud is. I can give you at present a metaphor only. Take the leading newspapers of our country, file them away day by day for a couple of hundred years, bind them into volumes without reference to time or place, and then commence to study from these books the history, laws, and customs of our country. For a long time the opinions of the ancient rabbies, as laid down in the Talmud, were considered valid and binding; our time, however, claims that we ought to know as much about the works of our present time as they knew about theirs, and as we may be incompetent to-day to legislate for the past and the remote future, thus have our wise ancestors been incompetent to provide for us. In a word, we claim the same right which they claimed at their time to provide for the present needs.

This again materially changes the ceremonial part of our religion. Another change which of late has taken place is, that we have given up all our claims to political existence. It took a long time before the land of our forefathers was forgotten. The persecution under which Israel suffered for many long centuries, the limited geographical knowledge which was possessed by all people, made us sigh and long for a restoration of the old country. But this phantom of political independence has vanished entirely. Modern Judaism has torn up the old titles which it held on Palestine. We hold to-day that we are the true sons of that country in which we live, and which protects our liberties and our rights; and if a few obsolete prayers referring to the old hope still linger in some old prayer-books, it is merely on account of conservative instincts, if not of ignorance of their meaning. It matters, indeed, little whether the prayers for the re-establishment of the Jewish nationality are rehearsed by our orthodox brethren, they are no longer even a true expression of their hopes.

Modern Judaism is by no means indifferentism. It means work. It acknowledges the historic mission of Israel to be the banner-bearer of truth and to proclaim to the world the doctrine of one God and one humanity. It claims that he worships God the Heavenly Father best who bears in his heart the greatest love for His children, and manifests the same by deeds of charity. Modern Judaism endeavors to foster in the hearts of the rising generation the pride of being Israelites, by removing all such empty customs, which would lower us in the estimation of intelligent men, without profiting our religion. Only he who believes in the immortality of Judaism, and is proud of being a son of Israel, can enter with enthusiasm upon the noble work in store for us.

In a word, all those who love Judaism are modern Israelites; all those who join in the glorious mission of Israel are believers in modern Judaism.

XIV.

THE SINAITIC REVELATION.

WHETHER it is on account of the weakness of the human mind, or on account of its strength, I cannot tell; but it is a fact that our intellect loves to wed events with places, buildings, and objects of every kind and description. The latter, insignificant as they are in themselves, gain by this marriage at once the respect and the reverence of the world, which otherwise they would never have been able to command, and the former receive in exchange a stronger grip upon the memory of men than they otherwise would have had force enough to obtain. Both events and objects are winners by their union. The old rusty sword, for which the junk-dealer would have hardly paid a penny, becomes at once a valuable object, and is placed on exhibition, because some celebrated general brandished it on a certain memorable occasion. The site of the house where Benjamin Franklin was born, the place where Warren fell, the tree under which Napoleon met with Bismarck after the battle of Sedan, the cannon from which the first shot was fired upon Fort Sumter, — all these places and objects, as well as a thousand others, which in themselves are of no value whatever, rise at once in esteem on account of the events connected with them, while the historical fact receives new force and is revived with new strength in the mind of the public at the sight of these relics.

About in the centre of the peninsula which stretches between the horns of the Red Sea, lies a wedge of granite rock rising from eight to nine thousand feet above the level of the sea. Its scenery is far from being picturesque, its usefulness to agriculture amounts to little or nothing; not even from a strategical point of view is that mountain-ridge remarkable. Its height is far from awe-inspiring, there is not the least trace of a volcanic eruption, which at some distant time might have produced such grand and terrifying scenes as Mount Vesuvius does from time to time; not even a river of some importance is born within its domain. This very mountain wedge, however, has become more renowned and celebrated than any other mountain in the world, its name has become more familiar to the human tongue than that of any other place on earth, on account of an event which is said to have taken place about three thousand years ago on this very spot. Who, in the civilized world, has never heard of Mount Sinai and of the remarkable event to which its renown is due?

When, in the days of my childhood, I read the biblical description of the Sinaitic Revelation, I always imagined Mount Sinai to be a cone rising up to some height in the midst of the desert, sloping evenly down on all sides. Around it I saw the people of Israel pressing toward the fence which Moses had been commanded to erect around the base of the mountain, eager to witness the grand scene which was to occur. I saw Moses going up and down the mountain, now conversing with God, now with the people; I beheld him, the great man, at the summit, enveloped in dark overhanging clouds, from which lightnings were bursting forth with unwonted brilliancy; I heard the peals of the thunder which followed every flash, and out of the midst of the fire and from out the noise and turmoil of nature I heard the divine voice give forth the Decalogue: "I am the Lord thy God, who have brought thee out of the land of Egypt."

How I longed to see that remarkable spot! I imagined that I could find and discern every feature of the mountain, that I could draw the very line to which the people had been permitted to approach; yea, even that I could trace the footprints of Moses ascending and descending the mountain.

I cannot describe to you, my friends, my disappointment when for the first time I saw a true picture of Mount Sinai and read a geographical description of the place. This mountain range, with a circumference of many, many miles, with three peaks instead of one, with roads leading from village to village, with hills and slopes, with ravines and valleys, this was not the Mount Sinai which I had imagined. Why, it must have taken Moses a whole day, if not longer, to ascend this mountain, and, according to the Bible, he ascended it twice on the same day, not speaking of the time his return to the people must have consumed. And when I furthermore read that amongst men of science it is still an open question upon which of the three peaks of Sinai the revelation took place, my belief in the literal narrative of the Bible suffered a severe shock.

Not until my experiences had multiplied; not until I had found that events wedded to some places or objects do not stand in any essential connection with them, and are by no means influenced and shaped by them; not until I had learned the lesson that their union is only fictitious, and is produced by our imagination solely; not until I had observed that a sword is a piece of iron, no matter by whom and on what occasion it was handled; not until I had lost faith in all relics, did I recover from that shock, did I understand that the Decalogue and Mount Sinai were not at all related with one another, that the one could not lose or win anything by its alliance with the other. The Decalogue is the most divine revelation to the human mind, no matter whether pronounced upon the summit of a mountain or in a valley, whether during the time of a storm or in pleasant weather, whether it was ratified by a large concourse of people, or originated in the soul of one man and had forced its way to general recognition and acceptation step by step, degree by degree.

We are assembled here to-night to commemorate not so much the time and the place of an event, but the event itself, which, in general parlance, is known as the Sinaitic Revelation. We have set this day apart as a festival of joy, as a day on which to rejoice that the light of reason has won a victory over the darkness of superstition ; that mankind has lifted itself from the low standard of the brute to the height of civilized humanity, by acknowledging the principle of law and order ; and that the first step in that direction was taken by our nation. The Decalogue in its entirety originated with the Israelites ; or, as we may say in other words, it has been revealed by God through the people of Israel.

To understand this in its liberal sense let us first examine what revelation means. A great many people have lost their faith in revealed religion, for no other reason than that they could not accept the coarse interpretation given to the word. The terms *revelation* and *discovery* are about synonymous; they cover about the same ground. Both presuppose an object which has always been in its place, but which has not been seen by us; both presume that at a certain time a certain hand pushed the curtain aside which stretched between us and the object and barred our way to it. There is only a slight difference between these two terms. Speaking of revelation we think that it was the hand of God which drew the veil aside; speaking of a discovery, we hold that it was the human hand which lifted the cover.

The coarse interpretation of revelation is that God, the invisible, made himself perceptible to the eye or the ear of some man or woman whom he selected for that purpose, and that he instructed them as to his will and wishes; that he pushed aside the veil which prevents man from seeing a truth, and showed him the path of life in bright daylight. The Sinaitic revelation, coarsely interpreted, means that God made his existence and presence felt in a peculiar way to the whole people of Israel, and that every Israelite, — man, woman, or child, — though they could not see any form, heard a divine voice, out of the midst of a column of fire, distinctly pronouncing what are known as the Ten Commandments.

The most refined conception of the word, however, coincides with that of the other term, with that of discovery: the divine hand leading the human hand to lift the curtain which hides the object for which we are in search. The distinction between the two terms has been kept up theoretically only; practically, we have arrived at the conclusion that every revelation has been a discovery, and that every discovery is a revelation. The story of the Sinaitic Revelation is to be taken by us as a poetical description, both of the grandeur and importance of the Decalogue, and of the impression which it made upon humanity; and, indeed, the writer remained far behind the actual revolutions and convulsions which these commandments have produced. To what does the peal of thunder, the flash of lightning, or the quaking of the earth, amount in comparison with the spiritual transformation of the human race, which began with the discovery of the ten principles upon which human welfare rests? Mankind had felt the existence of each of them singly long before, by instinct: some of them were no news to the people. And, indeed, they all must have been called into existence with mankind, as the laws of gravity, of electricity, and thousands of others, must have originated with the objects to which they refer; but they had not yet been understood: they had not yet been gathered into one common focus. Degree by degree the human race had to approach that light; and finally, a great man, born in a peculiarly gifted nation, was to tear away the last wraps which were hanging between it and mankind. Divine inspiration forced him to collect the scattered rocks and build of them a huge pedestal upon which the statue of human happiness could safely rest.

The Ten Commandments were not given to Israel alone; they were given through Israel to the world. The Ten Commandments are non-sectarian; they hold good for every race and denomination, for every century, for the past, present, and future, for every country, for every form of government, for every climate and every zone; they are a charter given to humanity at large.

There can be no doubt that the Ten Commandments are of divine origin; that they were enacted by the same supreme being who created the world and framed all the laws by which nature is governed. They have received acknowledgment these three thousand years; they have been adopted as the groundwork of all human legislation and religion : they have been tried at the poles of the earth and at the equator; and at no time or place has ever a change been needed. Not one of them has ever been abrogated or abolished; and what is still a greater proof of their divinity, no amendment to them has ever been thought of. We take some pride to-day in the wisdom of the framers of the constitution of this country; but barely one century has passed by, when we find that fifteen amendments have been needed, and consequently added to it.

If we to-day celebrate the great event of the Sinaitic Revelation, we do not celebrate it as Israelites merely, but as members of the human family; not for the sake of commemorating a supernatural, but a decidedly natural event. This festival is not a mere Jewish festival; it is a festival on which the whole world ought to rejoice, and in the celebration of which it will ultimately join.

The enemies of Judaism have frequently attempted to rob it of the fruits of its labors; and the claim that the Ten Commandments did not originate with the Israelites, but existed in part amongst other nations, is not a new one. But did not the law of gravitation exist long before Newton found a formula for it? Did not the laws which govern the electric current exist long before Franklin found a definition for them? Did not this continent exist before Columbus discovered it?

There is not one commandment of the ten which by right ought not to have governed the human race from its very start; but the grandeur of the Decalogue does not consist in the novelty of its laws, but in the completeness of their compilation; and, after all, only a few of these laws were known amongst the nations of antiquity. The acknowledgment of one God, the vanity of imagery, the necessity of one day's rest out of seven, the command to honor father and mother, and, above all, the prohibition of envy, the root of all evil, had never been pronounced before with such distinctness.

To sum it up: the Ten Commandments are coherent with humanity, they were born on the same day when the human race sprang into existence, they are of divine make and bear the stamp of the divine maker on their face, and we Israelites have no other claim on them than that our nation has been the medium through which the light has been spread over all the nations of the earth, that the Jews were the first discoverers and expounders of these remarkable laws.

But if they are of divine origin, and we, their discoverers, have been destined to be their guardians; if, furthermore, we rejoice to-day in that glorious mission, and assemble to celebrate an event of the greatest moment ever recorded in history, ought it not be our sacred duty at once to ascertain how near we have come to the realization of the wishes of God: how near we have come to the goal of human happiness marked by these very laws?

While suns and stars, the roaring thunder, and the destructive lightning, while all the forces of nature obediently and reverently bow before their Creator, and submit to the laws which he has given for their guidance, man alone keeps on revolting and rebelling against the divine will. For three thousand years the Ten Commandments have been the guide of humanity; but three thousand long years have not yet convinced the feeble being called man that his happiness and his woe depend on the obedience or disobedience to these laws. For three thousand years these beneficial laws have been known to man, and for three thousand years they have not been heeded.

Ah! my friends, we can easily learn these commandments by heart, we can easily imprint them upon the memory of our children; but to live up to them is quite another thing. What is the use of celebrating festivals in honor of these laws, of acknowledging their divinity, if in our daily life we act contrary to their commands, if we are unmindful of the lesson which they instil?

For three thousand years it has been known to the world that there is but one God; but behold how difficult it is for some of our most enlightened contemporaries to tear themselves from a threefold God and for others from the shallows of atheism? Three thousand years ago the law was promulgated, "Thou shalt have no other gods besides me," and behold people are still worshipping the vanities of life, — Gold, Power, Honor, — to the exclusion of the true God. For three thousand years mankind has been experimenting with the Sabbath question, and the wisest and best men of all religions have conceded that one day of rest out of seven, exactly as provided by the fourth commandment, is needed for the welfare of humanity; and still the Sabbath is ignored. You work seven full days in seven; and if it only were possible, you would work eight. For three thousand years the commandment, "Honor thy father and mother" has been taught by every parent to the rising generation, but alas! theoretically only, not practically. For if every man had honored his father and mother, the sad experience would not press itself daily upon us that fathers or mothers can raise seven children, while as many children cannot support one father or mother in their old age.

The commandment, "Thou shalt not kill," is three thousand years old, but behold the most flourishing factories in the world are those where instruments of war are forged, and the fat of almost every country is consumed by large standing armies of trained men-slayers, more courteously called soldiers. "Thou shalt not steal" is another of the divine laws by which human society would surely be benefited, but our prisons are overflowing, not to speak of those thieves who manage to evade the arm of human justice.

Nor during these three thousand years has the slanderous tongue been silenced, or the envious eye been blinded.

At first sight it seems as if these ten commandments had been a failure, because every one of them is boldly broken by us; but alas, what fools these mortals be! We do not see that a law stands high as a law, no matter whether it is obeyed or not; we do not see that all human misery, all our anguish and agonies of life, all our mortifications, are the consequences of and the punishment for our disobedience to these very laws.

Divine laws need no police to enforce them; their punishment of the disobedient rests with them. They protect themselves automatically against infringement.

Let us therefore not allow this remarkable day to pass by without reflecting earnestly upon the grand lesson which it instils. Ten commandments, so simple that every child can understand them, have been given to humanity. On our obedience to them depends our happiness and that of our children. They are not the whims of an irritable God, they are not the property of one sect or race: they are universal and endorsed by common sense as well as by an experience of three thousand years. Let us not ignore them: let us live up to their full meaning. Let us show to the world that to observe these commandments involves no hardship, no self-denial, no abnegation whatever. Let us prove to the world that the Jew is still the guardian of these laws and is benefited by their strict observation. These ten commandments are the foundation of Judaism, they will or can never be changed; but they are at the same time the foundation of humanity, and Judaism therefore will and must exist until all mankind shall have submitted to these laws. It is with us to shorten the time which lies between us and the age when all nations shall form one large family, and the festival of to-day calls upon us to fulfil our duty; namely, to propagate these ten commandments — not as articles of creed, but as living deeds; not as theories, but as practical achievements; not one or some as we may select them, but all in their entirety.

As the summit of this tabernacle is adorned with the two tablets containing the Ten Commandments, as such two tablets crown the edifice of this temple without, so must these ten commandments tower above all our innermost thoughts and outward actions, and their strict performance be the ornament and the most precious crown of our life.

This is the lesson of our festival to-day, this the result which ought to come from the commemoration of the Sinaitic Revelation.

XV.

MOSES.

AN inventive genius is said to have constructed a machine which not only had the appearance of a man, but could walk, talk, eat, drink, work, and act automatically like a man. He is said to have finished this man-machine in the best style, and so similar to a real man that, after it had been set in motion, it moved amongst men for years, without ever being detected as a counterfeit.

After a few weeks of intercourse with real human beings, the man-machine, however, became dissatisfied with itself: it perceived that its master had forgotten to supply it with a soul; and it wanted a soul. Day after day, from early dawn to the hours of night, it would plague him for a soul. The master finally tired of it, and, wishing to avoid his tormentor, removed to other quarters. But the very next morning the artificial man would enter his room, with the words: "Please, sir, give me a soul."

It was of no avail that he removed to another city, that he hid himself in obscure villages; the machine would find his hiding-places, and was sure to approach him with the words: "Please, sir, give me a soul." He resolved at length to place several thousand miles of sea between himself and his creature, and went to Australia. "I shall now be at rest," thought he, when he sat down at the breakfast-table in his hotel in Sydney. But he had scarcely touched the meal before him, when the door opened, and his machine, hat in hand, and humbly bowing, respectfully approached him: "Good morning, sir; please give me a soul."

The absurdity of this anecdote lies in the impossibility of constructing such a machine, of creating a body which would crave a soul; but turn the table, and you will find that almost daily in every one of us souls are created which constantly follow us with the demand: "Please give us a body." You will find that it is utterly impossible for you to escape these tormentors; that they will travel with you, cross oceans and deserts with you; and that there is nothing left for you but to give them the body which they demand.

There are souls which have no vitality whatever, and, therefore, die soon after their birth; there are others, however, who enjoy a healthier constitution, and struggle with one another for preference; and there are still others of such strength and vigor that the man who is haunted by one of them is compelled to sacrifice all that is near and dear to him — his time, his personal happiness, his family connections, his prosperity, his health, yea, often his life, — in the work of constructing a body for that soul.

To speak more plainly, every idea, every wish, which, like a spark of fire, flits up in our heart, is such a soul. They all crave a body — realization. Some of our wishes die in the very hour of their birth; they are those foolish wishes, which either are of no momentum, or are easily realized. If you wish for a new garment, a new book, a new ornament, or a new toy, and you have the means of giving a body to such a soul, you can easily rid yourselves of it; but there are wishes which are of momentum, and the realization of which is not so easy. They will follow you wherever you go; they will torment you constantly; they will enter your dreams, and disturb your nightly repose. They are the wishes which refer to the improvement of our worldly affairs, to the bettering of our present condition, to the gratification of our ambition.

Every man wishes to enlarge the circle of his usefulness, to build up his business, to become famous; and these are legitimate wishes, souls of a legitimate birth. They, too, crave realization; and in your efforts to supply them with a body, your best years pass by,—yea, your whole life is spent.

But there are souls of still greater dimensions, before which all the rest must give way; they are the great ideas, which are born in the minds of great men; ideas which encompass the welfare of all humanity, and the realization of which therefore is so difficult that it seems well nigh impossible.

Read the biographies of all the great men who have ever lived on earth, who have spent their lives in the service of humanity, and you will find that all have the same features in common.

A grand idea of universal importance flashes through their mind; a great soul is born to them, and this idea, this soul, haunts them day and night through all their life. In vain do they attempt to throw the burden from their shoulders, in vain do they attempt to escape their persecutors; the idea, craving realization, follows them, pitifully begging: "Please, sir, give me a body," and they must return to their duty, whether they will or not; they must plan, and prepare, and form, and carve a body for that soul. Suffering from the ingratitude of the world, despised, ridiculed, persecuted, on account of their strange work, now rejoicing, now despairing, now surrounded by flatterers, now forsaken by their best friends, they must toil on. The divine model stands before them; and after its pattern they cut, and carve, and chisel a body so great, so harmonious, so beautiful, that the world, after thousands of generations, is still bound to admire their skill, to bend the knee before their great genius, to love them for all the self-denials and sufferings which they have undergone so patiently.

Assembling here to-night, celebrating the Passover Festival, we evidently wish to pay our tribute of admiration to one of the greatest benefactors of humanity, to appreciate his services, to manifest the love which we bear to him on account of all his struggles and self-denials. Although Judaism has never idolized or deified a man, although it has ever claimed that adoration is due to God alone, we cannot celebrate this festival without remembering our great teacher and lawgiver, Moses; the man who has not only given birth to one of the grandest ideas ever produced by a mortal, but who spent his whole life in framing a body for this soul, a body of such greatness that it still towers above similar structures; of such strength that it has outlived similar creations; of such harmony and beauty that other masters have modelled their works after its pattern without ever reaching the original.

I do not propose to-night to revamp the history of Moses as narrated in the Bible. I hold that the writers of the Bible, in their simplicity, have not done him justice enough; they wrote a history of Moses the prophet, and not of Moses the man; they surrounded him with supernatural miracles and thus robbed him of the best fruits of his individual efforts. They wrote in the light and after the taste of their time: let us read between the lines, let us allow our imagination a freer scope, and let us review the life of this great man in the light and after the taste of our time. We shall arrive, however, at the same conclusions, though by a different route, namely, that every great man is the chosen instrument of God, and that every great idea which ever flashed upon the mind of such a man is a revelation of God, a soul, for which he was compelled to form a body.

At so great a distance of time, and without the necessary authentic sources to draw from, it is rather difficult to describe the earlier years of the life of Moses. The biblical record, though romantic and pleasing, does not satisfy us; modern criticism rebels against any miraculous intervention of God in human affairs. Romantic and pleasing the story is, indeed, that Moses was saved from a watery grave by the love of his mother, and then by the Princess of Egypt, that he was brought up at the royal court, and thus initiated in the wisdom of

Egypt; but it lacks probability. The princess would have shown great humanity, and would have been deserving of the greatest praise, if she had simply protected the life of the foundling, and had restored him to his family. In a country in which the spirit of caste prevailed to such a degree as in Egypt; in a country where customs and laws prohibited the entrance of a member of one caste into another, it must have been impossible even for á princess to introduce a member of the lowest, most degraded, and most despised of all castes into the highest and most respected, and for no other reason than that she had found the child years ago in the river. Granted that the momentary impulse of the princess when she found the child had been that of adopting it, we know only too well that afterthoughts, and especially a lapse of four or five years, change such impulses. But supposing even that he had been admitted into the royal household, how is it that the princess could not save her protégé when he had slain the Egyptian? Could her mighty influence not have secured the best lawyers for his defence? Could he not have been released on the plea of self-defence? And why had he to stay away from home, as the Bible tells, for forty long years, until all his enemies had died? Who were *all* his enemies?

Let us rather take things as they occur frequently and in reality: let us divest the facts of their romantic garment. In one of the lowest Egyptian castes, in a nation held in serfdom by the Egyptians, a bright boy is born, in humble surroundings. He grows up, and with him his inborn talents, his inborn genius. He sees what others do not see: he observes as others do not observe. Does he need a schooling? No! the whole universe is the school in which a genius is trained. The stars in the sky, the plants on the earth, the animals in the fields, the murmuring brooks, the surging sea, are his teachers. Great men seldom had teachers, and never needed any; their greatness is within them, and expands from within, like the bud of a rose.

Mediocrity needs teachers to evolve and bring forth the little talent which it contains, and which is too feeble to break forth of its own accord. A great man commands respect without being a scholar, and wields influence over others by his personal magnetism. Young Moses beheld the misery in which his nation lived: and the thought flashed upon him, "Free thy nation, break their fetters of slavery; for all men are alike, equal rights are due to all of them, and the enjoyment of freedom is the first and foremost of all human rights." The soul was born, and immediately craved a body.

He went amongst his brethren, preaching the

gospel of freedom, arousing them to break their chains, conspiring as revolutionists would do in our time against the government. The Egyptians soon learned to fear the young partisan, and persecuted him for high treason. Then came the critical moment. His own brethren denounced him. They were not yet ripe for a general uprising: they would not band together for the grand purpose. There were too many party quibbles amongst them; and when he undertook the part of a mediator between them they asked him jealously, "Who has made thee the judge over us?" They rather sided with their oppressors against him; and he was compelled to depart from his native soil, to abandon his cherished plans. He met with his first defeat.

Imagine, my friends, a young man of genius, full of enthusiasm for a great cause, struggling for the realization of a grand and glorious idea, endeavoring to form a body for the soul which once born in him would not leave him a moment's rest, but would torment him with the pitiful cry, "Give me a body." Imagine such a young man, defeated by his own friends, his well-laid plans thwarted by the indifference and the ignorance of those who were to be benefited by them, his hopes blighted, his works ruined, he himself outlawed and a fugitive, and you will understand why he dared not return before many years; you will understand who his enemies were.

Behold the difference! Which of the two is the greater man, Moses the petted favorite of a princess, sneaking away, a common murderer, or Moses the genial party-leader, the apostle of liberty, the political fugitive going into a self-chosen exile because of ill-success, leaving his country broken-hearted and in despair? Which of the two commands your admiration?

If you have ever met with a reverse of fortune, or with the ingratitude of those whom you loved best; if ever your plans miscarried; if ever you have stood before the ruins of a work the construction of which has cost you so much trouble and labor, you must remember the feeling of apathy which then took hold of you. "I shall never do it again," you would say; or, "This shall be a lesson for me," or whatever other expression of a similar meaning would burst from your angry lips. Moses had crossed the desert, he had found shelter amongst friends, and he was determined to withdraw from politics and to retire to private life. He fled from before the soul, but in vain. In Jethro's cabin, in the embraces of a loving wife, amidst the caresses of children born to him, he heard the cry of that soul, "Give me a body." With every year the cry grew louder and more pitiful. In vain did he remonstrate with his tormentor: "Who am I to undertake such work? Search for a better man! Who will ever believe me again after I have failed once?" But the voice kept on crying; the fire kept on burning, and the thornbush was never consumed. He struggled against it with all his might, but in vain. He had to submit; and he entered again upon the field of his former activity, this time to be successful and victorious.

The Bible tells us that he had lived with Jethro for forty years, but it contradicts itself on the spot by the statement that his second child was still a babe when he returned to Egypt; on the other hand, it makes it appear as if his transactions with Pharao, the ten plagues included, lasted only a few months.

The Bible, however, grand as it is in general outlines, is unreliable as to details; it cares little for the correctness of numbers or dates.

We may, therefore, accept it as very likely that Moses had remained with Jethro a few years only, but that between his return to Egypt and the liberation of the Israelites a long period of years must have elapsed.

He returned to Egypt better equipped and fitted for his mission than he ever had been before. The idea of freeing his nation had already assumed a more concrete form: it had grown larger, broader, deeper. The light had burst upon him that liberty cannot be cut to pieces and be dealt out in slices, one at a time. He knew now that he must grant either full liberty or none, that to be free politically without being free morally is an impossibility. He proclaimed, therefore, now, both liberty of body and of soul, both political and moral freedom. He was now ready to break both the fetters of serfdom and the bonds of superstition. He now stepped before his nation proclaiming one God and one common brotherhood.

Misery and exile had not crushed him; on the contrary, they had strengthened him; his genius had grown and its wings spread all over the moral horizon, covering and overshadowing every branch of legislation.

He began his work anew. Again he attempted to rouse his brethren, again he encountered their ignorance and indifference; but lo and behold! he made the king of Egypt listen.

It matters little how he accomplished his task; whether by the aid of supernatural miracles, or by political manœuvring; whether all the Israelites quitted Egypt in one night, or whether they left it — as is more probable — in single swarms and at different times; whether they remained for forty years in the desert, or whether it took forty years, more or less, before the different swarms of emigrants were safely settled in one part of Palestine; whether two and a half millions of Israelites departed from Egypt, or a number not so large as that.

All this matters little; the fact remains that the man Moses was the soul of the whole undertaking, that he organized, civilized, and colonized a nation of slaves, that he elaborated a constitution resting upon the principle: One God and one humanity. One God, the common father of mankind — all humanity one large brotherhood, every member entitled to enjoy equal rights, and an equal share of freedom and personal happiness.

This was the body which he created for his great idea, but not so easily was the work accomplished as described. Revolt after revolt had to be subdued, many a defeat had to be encountered, many a reverse of fortune had to be borne by him, and here behold the greatness of the man Moses. He has taken the lowest and most miserable of all Egyptian castes, he has torn it from the grasp of a mighty empire, he has colonized it in a country thickly settled with valiant foes, — he, all alone, without the help of any human being. But he has done still more; he has raised within a few years this degraded nation to the height of intelligence; he has made it the body-guard of the eternal truth that there is but one God, a God whom no human eye can see, no human ear can hear, no human finger can touch, but who nevertheless was, is, and will be,—a God who has created the world, preserves, and governs it; he has endowed this nation with laws before which after three thousand years the whole civilized world still bows in reverence; he has proclaimed through this nation to the whole world that all men are born free and equal, and that their life, liberty, and property must be kept sacred forever.

All this may appear trivial to us, who have been brought up amidst the blessings of his civilization, who have inherited his doctrines as a matter of course, who are accustomed to the liberty proclaimed by him; but three thousand years ago, when humanity was still enshrouded by the night of superstition; when idolatry of the coarsest character was still prevalent; when the right of the strongest was the only right maintained at the point of the sword; when slavery was sanctioned by law and custom,—at that time his laws and proclamations must have astonished the world; and I do not wonder at all, that, as it has been claimed, the mountains trembled and the earth quaked when he sent forth his message of universal freedom and equality, his proclamation of one God and one humanity.

Moses, like all great men, died a poor man. The services of great men can never be rewarded; and great men do not ask for compensation. Great men are, so to say, slaves. Moses, the proclaimer and champion of liberty, was a slave himself. He was the slave of the grand soul for which he was forming a body. All worldly considerations vanished before his grand task; they were too trivial, too diminutive, by the side of his great work. He had not time to think of his family.

Neither was Moses ambitious. Not even the spot is known upon which he closed his eyes for the last slumber. Great men are not ambitious; their own self dwindles into nothing by the side of the work for which they are commissioned. As they are forgetful of their family affairs so they are forgetful of themselves.

But, though no monument has ever been erected in his honor, though no festival ever was instituted to perpetuate his memory, he has never been forgotten. The names of great men are written with fiery letters in the book of life; and there we find, also, the name of Moses, with the qualification — the servant of God, the slave of his divine mission.

Of late a great deal has been spoken and written about the mistakes of Moses. Now, my friends, why should he not have made mistakes? Why should he have been an exception? Perhaps he has made more mistakes than you and I and Ingersoll dream of. Does the painter not erase many times a line which he has drawn, before he finds the one which suits his purpose? Does the sculptor not model and remodel a bust before he is satisfied with its form? After all, the mistakes with which he is burdened are not at all his mistakes; they were the mistakes of his biographers, the mistakes of historians of a much later period. But, supposing that they were his, what are they by the side of the great work which he left behind him?

Many men have entered upon their public career amidst the applause and the acclamation of the people amongst whom they lived. At an eventful crisis they have made themselves heard, on the crest of a political wave they have been lifted into prominence, but soon they have been carried away by the same wave, and quickly forgotten. Not so Moses. He has entered upon his career distrusted by all, unknown to all, the son of Amram; but his genius has cleared the way before him; he has compelled his adversaries to acknowledge his superiority, his talent, his skill, his faithfulness, and his integrity; and it is not before the end of his life that we find the nation listening to every one of his words, and obedient to every one of his dictates. This fact, if no other, shows to us that he must have been a great man indeed.

May the review of the eventful life of Moses, our great teacher and lawgiver, warm your hearts to love and revere not only his memory, but the work which he has constructed. May it fill your hearts with pride when you think of it that you are the guardians of his wonderful creation, that you are to preserve it, and to defend it against its foes.

Be true to your mission as he has been to his, and whenever an idea of general usefulness is born unto you, whenever such a soul asks you to supply it with a body, listen to it; do not shirk your duty; do not attempt to flee from before it, but accept gratefully the divine mandate, and devote yourselves to the task with all the energy that is within you. Our great Emerson says: "The one thing of value in the world is an active soul."

XVI.

PROPAGATION OF RELIGION.

ALTHOUGH the constitution of the United States of America does not recognize any distinction of creed whatsoever, and although objections have been frequently raised to the appellation "Christian country" whenever this term has been applied to the United States, it is an undeniable fact that after all this country is at present a "Christian country." Although a large number of Israelites are sharing with their fellow-citizens all the rights and privileges which this country so liberally grants to its inhabitants; although a number of Mohammedans, crowds of Buddhists, thousands of pagans, and even an uncounted multitude of pantheists and atheists, do dwell upon this hospitable continent, enjoying without molestation the rights of life, liberty, and of the pursuit of happiness,—there is no gainsaying that their combined number is so inconsiderably small in comparison with that of their Christian neighbors, which is so overwhelmingly large, that it would be folly to close one's eyes to the fact. Therefore I cannot but call this country a Christian country, on account of the vast majority of Christians living therein.

It cannot be denied, furthermore, that to a great extent our present civilization has evolved from Christian principles; we are surrounded from all sides by Christian customs and usages; our public schools, although they are claimed to be non-sectarian, are enshrouded by an atmosphere of Christian tendencies; take all in all, and you must concede that Christianity is a factor in life which it would be unwise to overlook in our calculations.

It may have occurred to many of you as an uncalled-for assumption on my part that I have touched of late so frequently upon a topic which so far has always been a *noli me tangere* (touch me not) of Jewish pulpit oratory; namely, that I have drawn Christianity into my discussions. On account of former persecutions the Israelites had inherited a certain timidity, and had become afraid to speak of the domineering religion, and to acquaint themselves with its teachings. The name of its founder was rarely, if ever, pronounced in a Jewish synagogue, and it appeared not only unnecessary, but even dangerous, to lay open the weak points of Christianity or to dwell on its strong ones. The consequence of this timidity was that we have remained absolutely ignorant in regard to Christian teachings, and that therefore we have become unable to discuss with our neighbors and friends the differences of our inherited creeds. Neither were we prepared to defend ourselves, nor could we lend a helping hand to our more liberal friends to root up old superstitions. While on every Sunday thousands of Christian pulpits have instructed large congregations as to the tenets of Judaism, with more or less accuracy; while the Christian clergy have made all possible efforts to enlighten their parishioners as to what Jews think and believe, the Jewish pulpit has remained culpably silent and the Jewish clergy have cowardly shirked their duty. I am well aware of it that when I first touched the sore spot many of my friends feared that lectures on such topics would create an ill-feeling against us in the community; but they had forgotten that times have changed. Religious intolerance is to-day in its last stages of decay, and, thanks to God, it has entirely disappeared in this blessed country. The pen has become mightier than the sword, and the press a more powerful engine than the cannon. The opinion of a man is respected provided he enters upon a research with love for truth, and unbiassed by prejudice. If we are to stand the pressure of Christian influence which is surrounding us from all sides, it would be poor policy on our part to close our eyes against it: on the contrary, it is advisable to familiarize ourselves with it, to examine it with the greatest care, and to show our friends at the same time what our opinions are concerning it. If Christianity of to-day is of a friendly disposition toward us, let us improve such friendship by the better knowledge of the friend; if it should be inimical to us, well, then, how could we better protect ourselves than by a thorough acquaintance with the forces which our opponent can lead against us? Let us therefore enter courageously upon such researches, but with love, unhampered by prejudice, and by all means with the respect and the courtesy which are due to the feelings of a neighbor and friend.

In the course of some other lecture I have asserted that paganism has never cared to spread its religion; that, to quote Gibbon here, all religions appeared to the masses as equally true, to the philosophers as equally absurd, and to the government as equally useful. Paganism, I said, lacked principles, a code of ethics, and a system, and therefore it has been unfit to impress the outsider. It could conquer, but not propagate itself. I have furthermore asserted that propagation of religion originated with Judaism, but that it was carried on negatively; that Judaism merely taught its lesson by example; and that, though it was always ready to receive a proselyte, provided he would join the fold thoroughly convinced of the goodness of its cause, and not for the sake of temporal benefit, it never invited the stranger, nor did it ever, as a rule, make converts by force or persuasion. The belief that God had made a covenant with their ancestors, to be binding for all future descendants, made it obligatory for them to teach the articles and clauses of this covenant to their children. Judaism was propagated directly only among the rising generation; indirectly, however, it was spread by the stubbornness with which the Jews refused to acknowledge the gods of other nations, or to permit any representation of the divinity to defile their country.

Christianity was the first religion which propagated itself in a direct manner, which adopted an aggressive policy in place of the defensive attitude of Judaism; and the marvellous success with which its efforts were crowned are to a great extent due to this change of tactics.

The success of Christianity is frequently used as an argument to prove its intrinsic truth. "Look at the enormous success of Christianity," say its adherents. "Could it have been achieved if the hand of God had not directly assisted it? Look at the success; could it have been achieved if its founder had not been a divine being? Look at the success; could it have been achieved if its ethics and principles had not been sound and true, and superior to those of Judaism?" Almost nothing is known authentically of the origin of Christianity; but whenever the identity of its founder or the reliability of its first sources is questioned, we receive always the same answer, "Look at the success."

Success, however, proves nothing. Success is a product of too many factors to prove by it the existence of a certain special number in its formation. Thirty-six is as equal to 4×9 as it is to 3×12, 6×6, or $3 \times 3 \times 2. \times 2$

Besides to its aggressive policy, the success of Christianity is due to the democracy of its principles. No matter how we may differ in our views in regard to its founder, we must acknowledge that Christianity has turned many Jewish theories into practical shape, that it has opened the avenues through which Jewish morals and Jewish ethics could exert their civilizing influence upon the pagan world.

While Judaism, proudly holding in its hand the divine truth, said to the nations of old, "Come to me, if you wish to walk by its light," Christianity carried it to them, and by persuasion and often by force compelled them to accept it, even against their will. Judaism had proclaimed to the world the doctrine that there is but one God, the common father of all mankind; but Christianity in its youth has practically stooped down to the ill-treated, despairing slave, and has told him that he was the equal of his master, and has treated him as such. The early days of Christianity, the time before it had defiled itself with pagan absurdities, will always command the admiration of all lovers of humanity. These early days are the period when it laid the foundation to its future greatness, and even to-day it can draw, and does draw, upon the resources which it had accumulated during the first three centuries of its existence.

To account for the marvellous growth of Christianity, we must familiarize ourselves with the conditions of that peculiar age.

Paganism had outlived its usefulness. The belief in many gods had lost its hold upon the masses, and idol-worship had fallen into disrepute. The past, so to say, had disappeared, and the future was not yet there. The struggles of the Jews, both with Greeks and Romans, had directed the attention of the world upon them; Jewish ethics had commanded the respect of the most profound thinkers of antiquity, the Bible had been translated, and the educated classes had become familiar with its sublime lessons. Politically, a large empire had been formed out of the countries of Europe, Asia, and Africa, extending from India to Great Britain, and from the Arabian desert to the banks of the Danube. Republican virtue had become extinct, and a wrangle between despots was now constantly disturbing the peace of the world. Corruption was flourishing at the capital and the provincial centres of the Roman Empire; extortion and degradation were its natural consequences. The social atmosphere was still more unhealthy. There were no middle classes: the free Roman citizen on the one hand, the slave on the other. To every free-born Roman ten slaves could be counted on an average. The small class of the freedmen could not adjust the scales. Years of prosperity had produced an extravagance and a luxury of which we can hardly form a conception. We turn with disgust from the description of a Lucullian repast, and our better feeling revolts against the obscene features of a Roman banquet. Dissipation on the one hand and misery on the other had made life unbearable; and suicides were of daily occurrence. Christianity found the pagan world rotten to the core, and thus a field of work as large as it was promising to yield a rich harvest to the one who would undertake to cultivate it.

If Christianity had been nothing else but a creed, a religious sect, which would speculate upon and discuss theological problems and theories; if it had established its church for no other purpose than to pray and sing therein; if its preachers had been merely paid officials, hired to entertain the visitor with flashes of oratory, it would never have prospered; the waves of time would have swept it away with the rest of philosophical schools which abounded at that time. But Christianity in its early days was more than a religious denomination; it was a political party, a socialistic organization; and its first efforts were flavored even with nihilism.

The Essenes, from which sect it had sprung, were pessimists of the first order. They did not believe in the future progress of humanity, but rather that, as the conditions of the time had become apparently unbearable, the whole world was on the eve of destruction, and that all would soon perish. Why should they therefore propagate their race by marriage, or hoard up capital for future use? The Essenes formed a socialistic brotherhood; they shared all property in common, and did not marry. To swell their numbers they were compelled to rely upon proselytes. They would approach a man, convince him of the soundness of their teachings, and initiate him into their order. The first Christians were Essenes. They opposed marriage, despised property, and were all in all a communistic brotherhood. Starting with the idea that their beloved master would soon return to hold judgment in a world filled with depravity, the first Christians considered it their duty to inform the whole world of the threatening catastrophe, in order to save as many as possible from the punishment which the justice of God was expected to mete out on that awful day. As they could reach only in rare cases the ear of the wealthy, they addressed themselves to the poor, to the slaves, to every one who was dissatisfied with the present state of affairs and was a sufferer from oppression. It was, indeed, good news and glad tidings to this class of people when they were told with all sincerity that the whole social order would be soon reversed, that the poor should become rich and the rich poor, that they should soon enjoy eternal happiness while their proud masters should suffer the well deserved punishment.

For almost three hundred years this hope was held out to the convert; for almost three hundred years the return of the master, the Messiah, the son of God, was daily expected; and all conversions were made under the promise that whosoever would join the new sect would not only escape the wrath of God on the day of judgment, but inherit eternal bliss. Every new convert became immediately a missionary; for he, too, had friends whom he loved, whom he could impress with his hopes and fears, and whom he wished to be saved on the day of judgment, and to share with him the benefactions which the new creed offered.

The entrance into the new society was made as easy as possible; the instructions were few; the ceremonies strange and impressive; and the persuasion of the missionaries so powerful, and so well calculated to appeal to the hopes and fears of every individual, that the organization could not but grow from day to day.

The new sect was at that time as vigorous and outspoken in its detestation of idol-worship as were the Jews; but it awakened the distrust of the government still more by its attempts to revolutionize the whole social order of the time. As I have said before, the early Christians formed small communities, the members of which shared all in common. They detested wealth and loved poverty; they not only preached abolition of slavery, but practised it. A convert to Christianity would at once set his slaves free; and, whenever a member had become a slave through the changing fortunes of war, his ransom was immediately paid by the next Christian congregation. Nor did the early Christians approve of war. Christianity originally abhorred it; and not before it had commenced to degenerate would it allow its members to carry arms. These communistic tendencies could not escape the eye of the government. The party in power was rather inclined to leave well enough alone; it disliked social experiments, and therefore attempted to suppress the rising danger by force. A country in which the majority of inhabitants were slaves, who were held in submission merely by the weight of custom, must have been hurt in its most vulnerable parts by the proclamation of so dangerous a doctrine as that preached and practised by the Christians.

It has been experienced more than a hundred times, that ideas cannot be killed by the sword, that the blood of martyrs is the best fertilizer for a new idea to grow upon, and that they will spread the quicker the greater the zeal is to suppress them. On account of persecution the early church was compelled to seek secrecy; but nothing is more attractive than secrecy. People do not care for things which every one can have; they crave the forbidden fruit. A sect which is granted the liberty of proclaiming its tenets by full daylight will never prosper; after the novelty of the thing is over, it will sink back into oblivion. But no sooner is a sect persecuted than the danger surrounding it works like a charm and attracts sympathetic friends; no sooner is a sect compelled to hide itself from before the eye of the government, than it grows in membership. The secrecy which was forced upon the early church became the cause of its success. It spread not only in spite of it, but on account of it. We have no authentic reports of what was carried on by the early Christians at their secret meetings. Their opponents and persecutors have charged them with immoral practices, which the Christians, however, have promptly denied. I could never believe in what Lucian tells of them, though by that time some impure elements might have already found their way into the originally pure society. The uniformity of their secret passwords, symbols, and tokens, the obedience with which the orders of their superiors were carried out, had the desirable effect that in any part of the world a friend and brother could be found and communicated with who would do his utmost to help a friend in distress. This was another and not slight advantage held out at a time when the highways were crowded with travellers, and travelling for pleasure or business had become almost as common as in our day.

There was, furthermore, a peculiar mixture of republicanism and despotism in the organization of the early church which guaranteed its success. The members of each congregation were at liberty to elect their officers, who in their türn elected a bishop for their diocese. This insured good officers, men who were worthy of the confidence of their constituency. But the congretion had no power to remove them afterwards from office, and was bound to abide submissively by their rulings. The dictatorial power of the princes of the church could accomplish more than otherwise would have been gained by republicanism pure and simple. The officers of the church did not only administer to the spiritual welfare of their flock, but for a long time they were the sole administrators of the common property. The richer a diocese was, the more important and influential became the office of a bishop, and thus these princes of the church left no stone unturned to enlarge their congregations by an addition of neophytes.

During the first three hundred years the same hereditary policy was adhered to until their secret organizations had spread and permeated all classes of society in such a manner that the Emperor Constantine was finally compelled to acknowledge them politically. With his conversion to Christianity we enter upon a new chapter in its history.

The church now changes its tactics. It feels strong enough to give weight to its moral persuasion by an appeal to physical force. The hope in the return of the master now disappears; the fear that the world will come to an end is now given up as childish; reward and punishment are removed into a world to come, beyond the clouds, beyond the tomb. In place of these primitive doctrines the firm resolution is established that paganism must go: that it is an act of piety to propagate religion even at the point of the sword. The former philanthropic and communistic schemes are laid aside as infeasible and impracticable ; marriage is made a sacrament, and the aspirations of the church run as high as to dream of the establishment of one large empire under the government of a prince of the church. Open war is now waged for more than three hundred years against paganism, and after the turmoil of the great migration of nations had subsided we find paganism at the feet of Christianity, its philosophical school closed, its temples either destroyed or converted into churches, and the star of the bishop of Rome in the ascendancy. He is recognized as the head of Christendom, the successor of the divine master, the representative of God upon earth. Kings and emperors bow submissively before his throne and receive their crowns from his hands. Christianity is now propagated by force of arms and the Christian priest now follows in the track of the Christian warrior, or *vice versa.*

During all this time Christianity had left Judaism unmolested, for several reasons. It had separated itself only by degrees from the maternal stock, and not before it had ascended the Roman throne with Constantine had it become polluted with pagan tendencies. From that time, however, it cuts loose entirely from Judaism, and we observe now how one dogma after the other is formed to suit the time, in flagrant contradiction to Jewish principles.

Too busy with its work of conquest, Christianity paid little attention to Judaism, nor did it fear it. With the exception of some theological controversy in regard to the nature of God, and some occasional legislation in regard to the celebration of Jewish holy-days, no efforts were made to convert the Jews by force or persuasion to Christianity. The Jews in their turn had become denationalized, and so intimidated by their recent misfortunes that they were satisfied to leave well enough alone; they carried on their trade, studied and expounded their law and propagated their religion, as before, only in a negative manner.

But when paganism had finally expired and Christianity had become the mistress of the world, when its dogmas and ceremonies had lost their original purity, and had become tainted with pagan customs and usages, when it was called upon to measure swords with a new enemy, Mohammedanism, and to wrestle with him for the championship of the world, it turned its eye towards the Jew, and wondered why it should wage an expensive war against the infidel Turks as long as in its own midst there was an element to be converted which so long had escaped its notice. From the time of the Crusades the pages of Jewish history show the marks of persecution, which was the outcome of a misplaced zeal on the part of Christianity to propagate its religion amongst the Jews.

The motives for this zeal, however, had changed. There was no longer the desire prevalent to save a friend from impending perdition, nor was the absurdity of idolatry to be contested. Political and social regeneration, too, was no longer intended, and self-preservation could no longer have been a stimulus for it. All attempts to convert Jews to Christianity were caused partly by jealousy, partly by greed. The Jews claimed to be the chosen people of God, and to have preserved the God-idea in its purity, and Christianity could not deny it; learned Christians knew rather too well that the trinitarian idea was no improvement on monotheism. Christianity had taught the pagan to abolish his idols; but the Jew now pointed with his finger at the images with which it decorated its churches, and at the idolatrous reverence which the masses paid to a host of saints.

While the meek Christian had turned a soldier and had won laurels on the battle-field, the formerly valiant Jew had laid the sword aside and had turned to commercial pursuits. His enterprise and his temperate habits had made him rich, while the warlike knights impoverished themselves by their indolence and extravagance. How could they rob the Jew of his well-earned property? They knew too well that he would rather part with his money than accept their semi-pagan religion, and therefore they threatened him with a forced conversion, in order to obtain his wealth. If they had earnestly undertaken the work of forcible conversion, not one Jew would have survived to tell the tale.

The modes of propagating Christianity among the Jews were in all countries about the same. They were placed under exceptional laws; they were compelled to debate with church authorities on religious topics, ostensibly to find the truth; they were prohibited to study their laws; their books were frequently delivered to the flames; the most absurd charges were brought against them, for example, that they would use human blood on the Passover Festival; exorbitant taxes were laid upon them; and occasionally they were expatriated. Spain, which most successfully propagated the Christian religion amongst the Jews, is still suffering from the consequences of her mistaken policy.

It was on account of these persecutions that the Jews became so disheartened, that they never thought of propagating their own views among their neighbors, that they feared every religious controversy, that they intrenched themselves behind distinguishing marks of all kinds, and that they were happy when forgotten by the outside world.

Time, however, has changed the relations between the two creeds. Science and a better knowledge of historical facts have relaxed the former prejudice, and the higher standard of morality and the more developed sense of justice have made such wholesale robbery as was carried on in former ages well nigh impossible. With it the zeal to convert the Jew has vanished. Our enlightened age has given up the notion that one religion only can be the right one, and that all the rest must be culpably wrong. The belief, too, has been abandoned that the performance of some ceremony constitutes religion. Beholding in every religion an attempt merely to grasp the infinite, we do not object to-day to a diversity of religious views, and grant to every religious system the right of propagating itself by lawful means.

If ever we should assert our right, and attempt to propagate Judaism, it must be with the full understanding that the forms of religion are not its spirit; that religion must be propagated neither by compulsion nor by intrigue, but by example; that we must convince, and not persuade; a conversion must never be made for the sake of temporal gain, but it must be the innermost conviction of the proselyte that our views of life harmonize with his own.

Divest both Christianity and Judaism of their mythological garments, reduce their history to facts and not to assertions which must be believed blindly, and you may rest assured that our arguments, our ethics and morals, will not be inferior to those of our neighbors, but must be the stronger as Christianity itself has been built upon the understructure of Judaism.

Allow me to close with a quotation from Professor Huxley: "What we are usually pleased to call religion nowadays is, for the most part, Hellenized Judaism. Not unfrequently the Hellenic element carries with it a mighty remnant of old-world paganism and a great infusion of the worst and weakest products of Greek scientific speculation, while fragments of Persian and Babylonian mythology burden the Judaic contribution to the common stock."

XVII.

CHURCHES AND THEIR RELATION TO MORALS.

TO both Jews and Christians, the small strip of land called Palestine, situated in Asia Minor, on the shore of the Mediterranean Sea, has been of more than common interest for thousands of years. In church parlance it was called the Holy Land. The imagination of pious worshippers was heated to such an extent that in many cases it became their most fervent wish to visit this land in preference to any other, to walk, at least once in their lives, the ground which their admired ancestors had trodden; to see the places upon which the reported supernatural events had occurred.

They imagined that the whole country was veiled in a mist of holiness, that the flowers therein were more fragrant, the water more delicious, the air more balmy, the animals more comely, sun and moon more brilliant than elsewhere. From the most ancient time down to ours, pilgrimages were made to these sacred spots: there was even a time when all Europe was infected with that travelling mania. I do not refer alone to the time of the Crusaders, when a war was waged for nearly two hundred years between Europe and Asia for the possession of these few square miles of land. No, even later the selfsame delusion prevailed amongst Jews and Gentiles.

Jehuda Halevi, renowned as one of the greatest poets of the Spanish period, a man of great wealth, who had filled the highest offices in the court of the King of Spain, had no greater ambition, no higher desire, than to behold with his own eyes the sacred places in Palestine. Not before he had reached a good old age was he able to realize his wish. Finally he laid down the honors and burdens of his various offices, settled his household affairs, and embarked for the Promised Land. While sitting upon the ruins of Jerusalem and bewailing the fate of the city he met with death at the hands of a common highwayman.

I know not whether these pious pilgrims were ever rewarded for their troubles by the sights they saw, but I think it must require a great deal of superheated imagination to find Palestine more interesting than any other spot on the globe. I cannot believe that the country of Palestine is holier than Massachusetts or any other. The waters of the Jordan are not different from those of the Charles River, and as for scenic effects there are thousands of places in this country and all over the world which surpass by far the natural beauty of the Holy Land. Neither do historic associations fill the scale in favor of Palestine. There is no spot on the earth where good and bad people have not lived, where humanity has not suffered and rejoiced, where stirring events have not happened, events which helped to civilize and advance the human race at their time and in their way, as did those which are reported to have occurred in Palestine. We meet with delusion and superstition in geography and history as well as in any other branch of science.

What Palestine was and is, historically or geographically, to the deluded pious, such is the church — or the churches, if you please — to the superficial observer in regard to morals.

Churches are believed to be the sole producers of morality; they are thought to be the only nurseries of morals; their representatives — priests, ministers, clergymen, rabbies, doctors, or by what other name you may choose to call them — are believed to hold a patent right on the manufacture of morals. But as Palestine is not more or less than any other country in the world, so does the church not wield greater power in the realms of morals than any other human institution, as, for instance, the home, the school, society, or the government. The church is *one* of the factors which by their multiplication produce morality, but it is by no means *the root of the product.*

Let us look upon a few facts which would astonish us if we were not accustomed to them by their daily occurrence. There is no institution split in so many factions as is the church; and, though all of these factions claim to strive for the same end, there is no deadlier enmity to be found in the factions of any other institution than that which exists between the different religious denominations. Liberty of conscience, as granted here and in some other countries, is only a truce which the contesting parties have been compelled to accept on account of their numerical weakness. Let one sect rise into strength and prominence, and liberty of conscience will soon become a dead letter.

Since the time that people assembled in public worship, or, in other words, since temples or churches were established, and priests, rabbies, ministers, or speakers assumed the moral government of the people, what a vast amount of good advice has been administered by them to their hearers, but with what effect? Have they become better on account of the many sermons addressed to them? Read the sermons or orations delivered by the ministers of all denominations from the time of Isaiah to the present day; what do they contain? What is their tenor? As a rule, they begin with praising the fidelity of bygone generations; they exalt the virtue and the moral standard of our ancestors; they seek for ideals amongst them alone, and find an everlasting supply. Then the prophet, preacher, or speaker will handle his contemporaries without gloves. To him, they are the worst generation that ever disgraced the earth. Religion with him is always on the decline; and if it were not for the hope that future generations would be better than the present, that our children were expected to return to the noble conduct of their great-grandparents, the speaker would despair of humanity, and see the only remedy of the evil in a second deluge. *Return* is the ever-repeated word of the church; you never hear the word *advance*.

This could be understood if the representatives of the church in a given generation had addressed their age in this manner because of the exceptional depravity of that generation; but what shall we say if there has never been a deviation from this style of harangue? Supposing we should be willing to return, should we be better off? Just read some sermons of fifty years ago. Just read what the church fifty years ago thought of the contemporary age; it was painted by its churchmen as black as ours is by the preachers of to-day, and so back through all the generations who have lived before us. Indeed, if we could read the exhortations of preachers a thousand of years hence, it would not be surprising if we should find exactly the same admonitions and exhortations, with the slight difference that our age would then be set up as an ideal, and our mode of living held out for emulation.

And, after all, who were the great promoters of humanity and civilization? Who were the men that shaped the morals of ages? Were they priests? Were they the representatives of the church? Not at all. Moses, the great lawgiver of our nation, the builder of the pyramid of morals around which our civilization solidly clusters, was neither a priest nor an orator. The founders of Christianity were no representatives of the established church of their time. Mohammed, the founder of Islam, was a business man. If the church is what it claims to be, the matrix of morals, how is it that it has never taken the initiative, that it has never revolutionized the moral world?

Carlyle says, "Man always worships something; always he sees the infinite shadowed forth in something finite." But how is it that, in spite of this craving for worship, people have never loved the church; that through the whole history of religion we find that people constantly and persistently act in opposition to the doctrines taught by the church. Scepticism and agnosticism are not children of our age; they are as old as the world is, they have always lived. They have been denounced by the churches of all ages, by Pagans, Jews, Christians, and Mohammedans; but there is no church which has not become possible on account of a preceding scepticism and a dissatisfaction with the previous church.

It is another fact that while the church never ceased criticising the moral conduct of the people, the people in retaliation were always distrustful of the church; and no sooner did one of the representatives of the church compromise the institution by improper conduct than a derisive scowl went through the land, denouncing the culprit and the whole institution with him. People were and are always ready for an innovation in church affairs, and those reformers who attacked the church of their time most fiercely were listened to with the greatest delight by the people.

Now, can you imagine that under such circumstances, laboring under so many disadvantages, the church could ever have monopolized the manufacture and propagation of morals? Could you for a moment imagine that under such unfavorable circumstances the church could ever have been in the van of civilization? The fact is that the church has not preceded but followed the march of civilization, that it has always accommodated itself to the demands of the time, that when people demanded reform, reform preachers arose, that it has not been the *mother* but the *nurse* of morality. Let us understand it well: the church is not the *originator, but the indicator* of morality. It shows at a glance outwardly how high the water of morality stands inside of the boiler of humanity. The water in the indicator always seeks the level of the water in the tank with which it is connected; it would therefore be a vain attempt to raise the water in the tank by a pressure upon the water in the gauge.

The church would be more efficient in its work when it should better understand its mission, which is to be the nurse of morals, and nothing else. Like a nurse the church must take the child under her supervision as soon as it is born, feed it with good and healthy food and protect it against evil influences, until it has become strong enough to take care of itself. She must forever be the faithful servant of its parent, humanity, and never assume to be its master. She must endeavor to win its confidence, improve and advance with it, but never retard its progress. She must ever change her dress and outward appearance at the command of her master; she must always look neat, clean, and tasty, in order to induce the parent to take the child from her lap to kiss and fondle it.

But let us now leave the metaphor to itself, let us rather build up an ideal church, such as should fulfil its mission and should be a centre of moral development, beloved, revered, and honored by all. I hope I need not explain that by the term church I do not understand the mere building, or a single denomination, but the whole institution, Jews and Gentiles, Catholics, Protestants, Mohammedans, Buddhists, flock and shepherd, pew, pulpit, and all.

Like a church-building the ideal church must be erected on solid ground. It must stand upon the rock of faith. Without the belief in a supreme being, in a God who is the omnipotent creator and preserver of the world, any church, no matter how tastefully decorated, must fall to ruin. The belief in God is one of the first and principal essentials of a church. If a congregation does not assemble for the sake of worshipping God, for what else does it congregate? Ethical instruction and social intercourse are worthy objects, but you can indulge in them outside of the church as well. You must first of all acknowledge that there is a God, that your life and prosperity are in his hands, and that you are under obligation to him. You must show your acknowledgment and gratitude to God by spiritual intercourse with him, as manifested by prayers and by such other demonstrations as in the view of the time would be pleasing to the father of mankind. A soul-stirring and soul-satisfying mode of worship is the first demand which must be supplied by the ideal church. Each form therein must have a meaning. Forms which have no longer any meaning, or the meaning of which is hidden in the mist of ages, must not be tolerated. Every worshipper, learned or not learned, talented or simple, old or young, must at once be impressed and enlightened by the ceremonial part of the service.

The ideal church must not look back too far into the past; nor must it look too far into the future. Its principal care must be for the present. We do not find all virtue in the past: nor will the future be immaculate; we must take our ideals from the present age. It is a mistake to undervalue our own moral standing. With a little less jealousy, with a little less prejudice, with a little less selfishness, we should find true manhood and womanhood in abundance around us from which to take our ideals. Allow me one illustration. Why, whenever we speak of republican virtue, must we always refer to the Roman general Cincinnatus, who laid down the highest position in the republic at the command of the people, and returned to his farm to raise turnips and carrots? Could we not just-as well teach it, and even with better effect, by pointing at the last two presidents of our republic, — Hayes and Arthur, — who, after their term of office, returned quietly to their desks in their law-offices? It is exactly the same in any other branch of life. We find Abrahams, Jobs, Davids, and Maccabees, in our present age as well. They never die out. It is a suicidal practice to exalt both past and future at the expense of the present.

Neither is it within the province of the church to solve geological, zoölogical, and astronomical problems. Leave these to the scientist, who makes a specialty of them. What has the church to do with the questions how the world was created, whether it took six days or six millions of years to form it, whether man was made of earth, or was the descendant of a lower species of animals. What business has the church to teach whether the sun moves or stands still, whether supernatural miracles occurred or not, whether Balaam's ass spoke or brayed? Suppose he spoke; what of it? Can these miracles give additional strength to the belief in God? Is not the growth of a blade of grass as much a miracle, and as unsolved a riddle to us as the reported passage of the Israelites through the Red Sea? Let the dead bury the dead. The church loses the confidence of its best adherents by not minding its own business, and by dabbling in all kinds of sciences. If a scientist makes a mistake it matters little; the next expert who proves the error will take his place until another proves him to be wrong; but the church cannot afford to be corrected: it loses immediately its hold upon the minds of its adherents. Our present indifferentism springs from no other source than the fact that geological and astronomical statements made and upheld by the church have been found to be erroneous. The ideal church must work for the present. Here we are, no matter how it came that we are here. Here is the world with its innumerable miracles. Here are our fellow-beings. What are we to them, and they to us? How must we act in order to live happily all together during the brief period granted to us? What are our relations to the great cause of the creation? These are the questions which the ideal church is called upon to treat; and I should think that there is enough in them to reflect upon, to search for, and to speak about.

Let the future, too, take care of itself. Need we trouble ourselves as to what mankind will be or do a thousand years from now? If we are to pave the way for its future prosperity, let us pave our section of the road; but we cannot be expected to pave the whole route.

The ideal church, furthermore, must teach, not criticise; it must speak the truth, but not insult; it must demand self-command, but not abnegation; it must encourage contentment, but not asceticism.

Allow me to point out a mistake which the churches of all denominations have made to the present day, and which the ideal church must avoid.

Though they acknowledged correctly the differences between spirit and flesh, they never recognized the rights of the flesh. They attempted to make man a spirit even before death. They never ceased in their vituperation and condemnation of the flesh. They took a delight in starving the body. Fasting was upheld as a sacred duty; and to break a fast was stigmatized as an unpardonable sin. The ideals, therefore, which they put up were totally impracticable. If all men were to live and to act like the saints of all churches, human society would soon fall to pieces; it could not exist. The churches demand too much from their devotees. A man cannot think constantly of God and of nothing else; nor can he constantly pray; neither can he devote all his time to church work. Spirit and flesh must work in harmony with each other. God created them both for their special duties; they are friends, and not, as the churches claim, antagonists.

The ideal church must work. It matters

little what the fundamental doctrines of any denomination are, as long as they work with the right purpose. The members of each denomination must ally themselves to one another for the purpose of working together in friendship and harmony for the preservation and development of morals. They must work for justice, truth, love, and charity, and not simply talk about them.

It is a pity that the Jewish church has been robbed of its effectiveness, and that its work has been reduced to almost nothing. Its founders had given it all the scope it wanted; formerly the Jewish church administered the law, instructed the young, and dispensed all charities, but later generations have taken away one province after the other from it.

With the loss of the political existence of our nation, the administration of the law was taken from it. Then the school had to be given up by necessity. Finally charity has been switched off from the congregation, and handed over to the orders and other charitable societies established for that special purpose. But it is a grave mistake. A church which does not *work* loses all its dignity and influence.

The ideal church must reconquer the lost provinces and give out work to every member, and indeed the field of charity alone is large enough to supply all. Charity is the principal work of the church, but, understand me rightly, charity is not the giving of alms, but the distribution of them; it is not a tax levied upon our pocketbook but upon our time, our brains, our intellect, and energy. Charity means to modify and to alleviate social evils, but not merely to fill the hands of all who hold them up to us, without discrimination. Charity requires work, earnest work, and the ideal church must organize and direct it.

Shall I say a word or two about the leaders of the ideal church? I believe in its republican form of government, I believe that it must be a church of the people, for the people, and by the people. I believe that its leaders, both secular and spiritual, should be practical men, and not merely theorists or linguists. They ought to understand political economy rather than the Chaldee language. They ought to be familiar with the history and the literature of their own time and country rather than with that of Hindostan or Persia.

Such a church, if established in every denomination, will soon become universal and unite all humanity in its fold. It is the church of the future, the church of the time which we expect to come and which we call the Messianic time. Let us pave our section of the road leading to it.

www.ingramcontent.com/pod-product-compliance
Lightning Source LLC
Chambersburg PA
CBHW032046230426
43672CB00009B/1494